GEORGIA TEST PREP

Mathematics Quiz Book

Georgia Milestones Mathematics

Grade 4

ISBN 978-1790891856

TEST MASTER PRESS

www.testmasterpress.com

CONTENTS

INTRODUCTION
For Parents, Teachers, and Tutors

About the Georgia Standards of Excellence

The state of Georgia has adopted the Georgia Standards of Excellence. These standards describe the skills that students are expected to have. Student learning is based on these standards throughout the year, and the Georgia Milestones tests assess these standards. This quiz book covers all the skills listed in the Georgia Standards of Excellence.

Developing Mathematics Skills

The Georgia Standards of Excellence require students to have a thorough and in-depth understanding of mathematics skills, as well as the ability to apply the skills to solve problems. To ensure that students have the abilities needed, the quizzes contain rigorous questions that require students to explain concepts, apply skills, complete tasks, or describe how a problem was solved. These advanced questions will ensure that students gain an in-depth understanding of the skills and have the ability to apply the skills to solve problems.

Completing the Quizzes

The quizzes are divided into the main subject areas, or domains, of the state standards. Within each section, there is one quiz for each specific skill that students need. For each quiz, the difficulty of questions increases from simple to complex. This format introduces the skill, and then encourages students to apply the skill and to develop complete understanding of the skill. Many quizzes also include guided questions that will help students understand what is expected in answers. This will ensure that students gain a thorough and complete understanding of each skill.

Preparing for the Georgia Milestones Mathematics Assessments

Students take the Georgia Milestones Mathematics assessment each year. The test is made up of around 70 questions that assess all the skills in the Georgia Standards of Excellence. The questions have a range of formats including selected-response, technology-enhanced, constructed response, and extended constructed response that may require students to complete a complex task, explain a concept, or justify an answer.

This quiz book will provide students with the knowledge and skills required to perform well on the assessments. Students will gain the mathematical knowledge that the tests measure. Students will gain the thorough understanding needed to show knowledge of the mathematics skills, as well as the ability to apply the skills to solve problems. Students will also have experience answering a wide range of question types. This will ensure that students have the skills, knowledge, and experience needed to perform well on the tests.

Quizzes 1 to 13

Operations and Algebraic Thinking

Directions

Read each question carefully. For each multiple-choice question, fill in the circle for the correct answer. For other types of questions, follow the directions given in the question.

You may use a ruler to help you answer questions. You should answer the questions without using a calculator.

MATHEMATICS SKILLS LIST
For Parents, Teachers, and Tutors

Quizzes 1 through 13 cover these skills from the Georgia Standards of Excellence.

Operations and Algebraic Thinking

Use the four operations with whole numbers to solve problems.

1. Understand that a multiplicative comparison is a situation in which one quantity is multiplied by a specified number to get another quantity.
    a. Interpret a multiplication equation as a comparison, e.g., interpret $35 = 5 \times 7$ as a statement that 35 is 5 times as many as 7 and 7 times as many as 5.
    b. Represent verbal statements of multiplicative comparisons as multiplication equations.

2. Multiply or divide to solve word problems involving multiplicative comparison. Use drawings and equations with a symbol for the unknown number to represent the problem, distinguishing multiplicative comparison from additive comparison.

3. Solve multistep word problems with whole numbers and having whole-number answers using the four operations, including problems in which remainders must be interpreted. Represent these problems using equations with a letter standing for the unknown quantity. Assess the reasonableness of answers using mental computation and estimation strategies including rounding.

Gain familiarity with factors and multiples.

4. Find all factor pairs for a whole number in the range 1-100. Recognize that a whole number is a multiple of each of its factors. Determine whether a given whole number in the range 1-100 is a multiple of a given one-digit number. Determine whether a given whole number in the range 1-100 is prime or composite.

Generate and analyze patterns.

5. Generate a number or shape pattern that follows a given rule. Identify apparent features of the pattern that were not explicit in the rule itself. Explain informally why the pattern will continue to develop in this way.

Quiz 1: Understanding Multiplication

1 Which situation can be represented by the equation $9 \times 6 = 54$?

&Ⓐ Ally saved $9 one week and $6 the next week.

Ⓑ Ally had $54 in savings left after spending $9.

Ⓒ Ally saved $9 each week for 6 weeks.

Ⓓ Ally spent $54 each month for 6 months.

2 Which of these is represented by the model below?

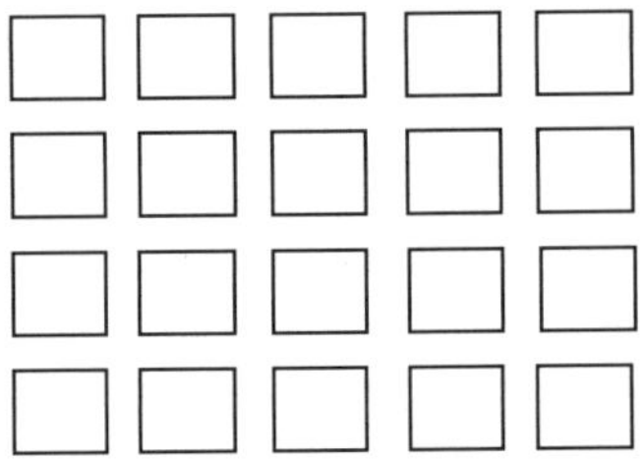

Ⓐ 20 is 4 times as many as 5

Ⓑ 40 is 2 times as many as 20

Ⓒ 5 is 4 times greater than 20

Ⓓ 4 is 20 times greater than 5

3 Dan and Leah placed coins in piles. Every pile had the same number of coins in it. Dan's piles are shown below.

Leah has 3 times as many piles as Dan. How many coins does Leah have?

Ⓐ 12   Ⓑ 24   Ⓒ 42   Ⓓ 72

4 Kimi found that her dog's mass was 4 times as much as her cat's mass. If her cat's mass was 8 kilograms, what was her dog's mass?

Ⓐ 2 kg   Ⓑ 12 kg   Ⓒ 32 kg   Ⓓ 48 kg

5 Complete each statement with two numbers that make the statement true. Then complete the equation to represent the statement.

14 is ___7___ times as many as ___2___ $14 = \underline{2} \times \underline{7}$

21 is ___7___ times as many as ___3___ $21 = \underline{3} \times \underline{7}$

35 is ___1___ times as many as ___5___ $35 = \underline{5} \times \underline{7}$

49 is ___7___ times as many as ___7___ $49 = \underline{7} \times \underline{7}$

55 is ___11___ times as many as ___5___ $55 = \underline{5} \times \underline{11}$

6 The table below shows how far students live from school.

Student	Wesley	Flynn	Gino	Thomas	Corey
Distance (miles)	2	6	18	30	?

Complete each statement below with the correct number.

Flynn lives ___4___ times as far from school as Wesley.

Gino lives ___16___ times as far from school as Wesley.

Thomas lives ___28___ times as far from school as Wesley.

Gino lives ___12___ times as far from school as Flynn.

Thomas lives ___24___ times as far from school as Flynn.

Corey lives 7 times as far from school as Flynn. How far does Corey live from school? ___42___ miles

7   Decide if each problem can be solved with addition or with multiplication. Circle the correct word to show your choice. Then write an expression that can be used to solve the problem. Write your answer on the line.

Hannah is 14. Oliver is 3 years older than Hannah. How old is Oliver?

(addition)   multiplication

Expression $\begin{array}{r} 14 \\ +3 \\ \hline 17 \end{array}$ **Answer** _17_ years old

A pound of peaches costs 5 times as much as a pound of apples. A pound of apples costs $3. How much does a pound of peaches cost?

addition   (multiplication)

Expression $\begin{array}{r} 5 \\ \times 3 \\ \hline 15 \end{array}$ **Answer** $ _15_

A new building has 5 times as many floors as the old building. The old building had 6 floors. How many floors does the new building have?

addition   (multiplication)

Expression $\begin{array}{r} 5 \\ \times 6 \\ \hline 30 \end{array}$ **Answer** _30_ floors

Fiona's new school has 15 more fourth grade students than her last school. Her last school had 80 fourth grade students. How many fourth grade students does her new school have?

(addition)   multiplication

Expression $\begin{array}{r} 80 \\ +15 \\ \hline 95 \end{array}$ **Answer** _95_ students

A store sold 18 cameras on Thursday and 4 times as many on Friday. How many cameras were sold on Friday?

addition   multiplication

Expression $\begin{array}{r} 18 \\ \times 4 \end{array}$ **Answer** _92_ cameras

8 Kim is buying notebooks for $3 each. She drew the diagram below to show how many notebooks she can buy for $12.

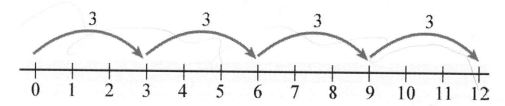

How many notebooks can she buy? __4__ notebooks

Explain how the diagram helped you find the answer.

I knew 3 × 4 = 12 and she had 12$ total.

9 Andre practiced speaking Spanish for 15 minutes each day for 5 days. How long did he practice for in all? Show how to find the answer on the number line below. Then write the answer on the line.

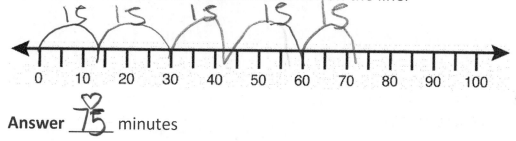

Answer __75__ minutes

10 Delvina has $20 in savings. She needs 4 times as much to buy a camera. How much does she need to buy the camera? Show how to find the answer on the number line below. Then write the answer on the line.

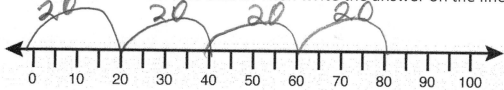

Answer $ __80__

Quiz 2: Using Multiplication Equations

1   Which situation can be represented by the equation $12 \times 7 = 84$?

Ⓐ Taylor rode 12 miles every day for 7 days.

Ⓑ Taylor bought his bike for $84 and a helmet for $7.

Ⓒ After riding 12 miles, Taylor had 7 miles left to ride.

Ⓓ In a race of 84 people, 12 people didn't finish the race.

2   Which statement is represented by the equation below?

$$25 \times 5 = 125$$

Ⓐ The number 25 is 5 less than 125.

Ⓑ The number 25 is 5 times as many as 125.

Ⓒ The number 125 is 5 more than 25.

Ⓓ The number 125 is 5 times as many as 25.

3   A delivery person has 3 boxes of equal mass. He places 1 box on the first trolley, and 2 boxes on the second trolley.

If the mass of the box on the first trolley is m, which expression represents the mass of the boxes on the second trolley?

Ⓐ $2 + m$ Ⓑ $2 \times m$ Ⓒ $m \div 2$ Ⓓ $2 - m$

4   Ryan's uncle is 36. Ryan's uncle is 3 times older than Ryan. Which equation can be used to find Ryan's age, r?

Ⓐ $3 \div r = 36$ Ⓑ $3 \times r = 36$ Ⓒ $r \div 3 = 36$ Ⓓ $3 \times 36 = r$

5 Danielle sold 20 necklaces. She sold 4 times as many bracelets. Which of these are ways to find how many bracelets she sold? Select all the correct answers.

☐ 20 + 4 = ?   ☒ 20 × 4 = ?

☒ 20 + 20 + 20 + 20 = ?   ☐ 20 − 4 = ?

☐ 4(20) = ?   ☒ 4(20 + 4) = ?

6 A rug has a length, *l*, that is 3 times its width, *w*. Which of these could be used to find the length of the rug? Select all the correct answers.

☐ 3*w*   ☐ *w* - 3

☐ *w* × *w* × *w*   ☒ *w* + *w* + *w*

☒ *w* + 3   ☐ 3 + *w* + *w*

7 Write and solve a multiplication expression to answer each question.

Jane has 6 rows of 8 stickers. How many stickers does she have in all?

$\underline{6} \times \underline{8} = \underline{48}$ **Answer** $\underline{48}$ stickers

There are 9 bowls of 4 apples each. How many apples are there in all?

$\underline{9} \times \underline{4} = \underline{36}$ **Answer** $\underline{36}$ apples

Lydia earns $12 each hour she works. How much does she earn in 8 hours?

$\underline{12} \times \underline{8} = \underline{96}$ **Answer** $\underline{96}$

Eric buys 5 tickets for $15 each. How many dollars does he spend in all?

$\underline{5} \times \underline{15} = \underline{75}$ **Answer** $\underline{75}$

Arty drives at 60 miles per hour. How far does he drive in 3 hours?

$\underline{60} \times \underline{3} = \underline{180}$ **Answer** $\underline{180}$ miles

8 Write and solve a multiplication expression to answer each question.

Mia has 7 times as many baseball cards as Carolyn. Carolyn has 4 baseball cards. How many baseball cards does Mia have?

__7__ × __4__ = __28__   **Answer** __28__ baseball cards

Rocco served 6 aces in a tennis match. Shane served 3 times as many aces in the match as Rocco. How many aces did Shane serve?

__6__ × __3__ = __18__   **Answer** __18__ aces

Mr. Pearce thought his drive to work would take 15 minutes. Due to traffic, it took 4 times longer than he thought. How long did the drive take?

__4__ × __15__ = __60__   **Answer** __60__ minutes

Celeste saved $12 in January. She saved 5 times as much in February. How much did she save in February?

__12__ × __5__ = __60__   **Answer** $ __60__

Anderson bought 4 notebooks. He bought 6 times as many pens as notebooks. How many pens did he buy?

__6__ × __4__ = __24__   **Answer** __24__ pens

9 Jordana bought 4 packets of cookies. There were an equal number of cookies in each packet. She bought a total of 24 cookies. Complete the equation that can be used to find the number of cookies in each packet, n. Then solve the equation.   4×6=24

Equation __4__ × n = __24__   **Answer** __24__ cookies

Jordana spent a total of $12 on the 4 packets. Complete the equation that can be used to find the cost of each packet, c. Then solve the equation.

Equation __4__ × c = __12__   **Answer** $ __12__

10 Daniel packed 72 soda cans into boxes. He placed 6 soda cans in each box. Write and solve an equation to find the number of boxes he used, *b*.

$$6 \times b = 72$$
$$6 \times 12 = 72$$

Answer _12_ boxes

11 Anthony is 8 years old. Anthony is 4 times as old as Gina. Write and solve an equation to find Gina's age, *g*.

$$8 \times 4 = G$$
$$8 \times 4 = 32$$

Answer _32_ years old

12 A standard batch of muffins makes 12 muffins. Mrs. Henry made a batch that was 4 times the size of a standard batch. Write and solve an equation to find the number of muffins she made, *m*.

Show your work.

$$12 \times 4 = m$$
$$12 \times 4 = 48$$

	10	2
4	40	8

Answer _48_ muffins

13 Ivan scored 3 points in his first basketball game. He scored 4 times as many points in his second game as his first game. He scored 6 times as many points in his third game than his first game. Write and solve equations to find how many points, *p*, he scored in his second and third games. Then find the total number of points he scored in his first three games.

$$3 \times 4 = 12$$
$$3 \times 6 = 18$$
$$30$$

Answer Game 2 _12_ pts, Game 3 _18_ pts, Games 1 to 3 _30_ pts

Quiz 3: Using Multiplication to Solve Problems

1   Louisa is making fruit punch. She pours 4 cartons of orange juice into the punch. Each carton contains 12 ounces of orange juice. How many ounces of orange juice are in the punch?

$4 \times 12 = 48$

   Ⓐ 46 oz   Ⓑ 48 oz   © 52 oz   Ⓓ 58 oz

2   Alex saw the sign below at a fruit stand.

Apples
15 for $1

$3 \times 15 = 45$

If Alex spent $3 on apples, how many apples would he get?

   Ⓐ 30   Ⓑ 35   © 45   Ⓓ 60

3   A music school divided its students into 5 classes. There were 19 students in each class. How many students were there in all?

$19 \times 5 = 45$

   Ⓐ 38   Ⓑ 55   © 90   Ⓓ 95

4   Jared has 21 baseball cards. Milo has 3 times as many baseball cards as Jared. How many baseball cards does Milo have?

$21 \times 3 = 63$

   Ⓐ 7   Ⓑ 18   © 24   Ⓓ 63

5   A rectangle has a width that is 4 times its length. Which of these could be the dimensions of the rectangle? Select all the possible answers.

   ☑ 16 cm long, 4 cm wide   ☐ 18 cm long, 22 cm wide

   ☐ 3 cm long, 12 cm wide   ☑ 24 cm long, 6 cm wide

   ☐ 14 cm long, 18 cm wide   ☐ 5 cm long, 20 cm wide

   ☐ 6 cm long, 10 cm wide   ☑ 8 cm long, 4 cm wide

6 A store sells small juices for $3 each, medium juices for $4 each, and large juices for $5 each. Write 1, 2, 3, and 4 on the lines to place the orders from lowest cost to highest cost.

_4_ 8 small juices and 4 large juices

_2_ 6 medium juices and 3 large juices

_3_ 2 small juices and 7 large juices

_1_ 4 small juices, 2 medium juices, and 3 large juices

(handwritten: 3x8=24 > 44; 4x5=20; 5x3=15 > 39; 6x4=24; 3x2=6; 7x5=35; 41; 4x3=12; 2x4=8; 3x5=15 > 35)

7 Four sisters did odd jobs on the weekend and were paid in quarters. The table shows how many quarters they earned. Complete the table with the value of each sister's quarters.

Name	Beverly	Andrea	Nicky	Blair
Number of Quarters	8	28	20	12
Total Value (cents)	200	700	500	300
Total Value ($)	2$	7$	5$	3$

8 A restaurant makes 18 apple pies. Each pie is cut into 8 pieces and each piece is sold for $3. How much would be made if all the pieces were sold?

Show your work.

(handwritten: 18x8=; 8 | 80 | 64; 144x3; 100 40 4; 3 | 300 | 120 | 12)

Answer $ _432_

9 Kym is buying cotton and lace to make curtains. The cotton costs $12 per yard and the lace costs $8 per yard. Kym buys 16 yards of cotton and 6 yards of lace. How much would Kym pay for the cotton and lace?

Show your work.

(handwritten: 12x16; 10 | 200 | 20; 6 | 60 | 12; 8x16=48; 292; +48; 340)

Answer $ _340_

10   Jane sorted the coins she had into groups to count them. Jane wrote this list to describe her coins.

- There are 6 quarters.
- There are 3 times as many dimes as quarters.
- There are 4 times as many nickels as dimes.
- There are 10 times as many pennies as quarters.

Find the number of coins of each type Jane has.

Show your work.

6q $6 \times 3 = 18$ $4 | 48 | 32$
18d $18 \times 4 = 80$
80 n
800 p $80 \times 10 = 800$

Answer _6_ quarters, _18_ dimes, _80_ nickels, _800_ pennies

11   Stefan's basketball team scored 18 points in the first half of the game. The team scored 3 times as many points in the second half. What was the total number of points scored?

Show your work.

$18 \times 3 = 54$

$3 | 30 | 24$

Answer _54_ points

Stefan scored 7 of the total points. Luke scored 6 times as many total points as Stefan. How many points did Luke score?

Show your work.

$7 \times 6 = 42$

Answer _42_ points

12 Austen's phone bill was $16 in January. It was 3 times as much in February as in January. It was 2 times as much in March as in February. What was Austen's total phone bill for the three months?

Show your work.

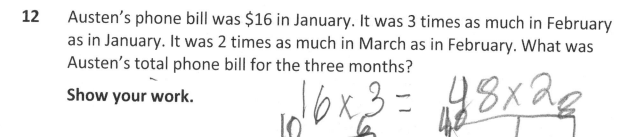

Answer $ 96

13 Madeline made a quilt by sewing square pieces of material together. The first row of her quilt is shown below.

Madeline made a quilt that was 4 rows wide. How many pieces of material did Madeline use?

Show your work.

$8 \times 4 = 32$

Answer 32 pieces

Madeline then decided to make the quilt 2 times as long and 3 times as wide. How many pieces of material would be used to make this quilt?

Show your work.

$32 \times 2 = 64$

$64 \times 3 = 192$

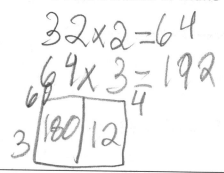

Answer 192 pieces

Quiz 4: Using Division to Solve Problems

1   Jo has 18 star-shaped stickers. He places them in rows of 6 stickers each.

Which expression represents how many rows of stickers he would have?

Ⓐ 18 × 6   Ⓑ 18 ÷ 6   Ⓒ 18 - 6   Ⓓ 18 + 6

2   Winona has 48 stamps. She has 6 times as many stamps as Catherine. How many stamps does Catherine have?

Ⓐ 8   Ⓑ 12   Ⓒ 42   Ⓓ 288

3   Portia has 24 books she wants to read in 6 months.

If she reads an equal number of books each month, how many books does she need to read each month?

Answer ___4___ books

4   Which of these would have 8 students in each team? Select all the correct answers.

☑ 40 boys and 32 girls divided into 9 equal teams

☐ 56 boys and 24 girls divided into 7 equal teams

☐ 20 boys and 60 girls divided into 8 equal teams

☐ 45 boys and 35 girls divided into 10 equal teams

☑ 45 boys and 54 girls divided into 11 equal teams

☑ 42 boys and 54 girls divided into 12 equal teams

5   Mr. Wade needs to place 84 students in equal groups. He decides he could have 2, 3, 4, 6, or 7 equal groups. Complete the table to show the number of students that will be in each number of groups.

Number of Groups	Calculation	Number of Students in Each Group
2	84 ÷ 2	42
3	84 ÷ 3	28
4	84 ÷ 4	22
6	84 ÷ 6	14
7	84 ÷ 7	12

6   Write and solve a division expression to answer each question.

April sorts 70 dimes into 5 equal piles. How many dimes are in each pile?

$70 \div 5 = 14$ **Answer** 14 dimes

A packet of 8 bagels costs $24. What is the cost of each bagel, in dollars?

$24 \div 8 = 3$ **Answer** $ 3

Bo washes cars for $9 each and makes $108. How many cars did he wash?

$108 \div 9 = 12$ **Answer** 12 cars

There are 8 limes per bag. Jed buys 48 limes. How many bags did he buy?

$48 \div 8 = 6$ **Answer** 6 bags

A teacher divides 96 students equally between 3 buses. How many students are on each bus?

$96 \div 3 = 32$ **Answer** 32 students

7 Write and solve a division expression to answer each question.

Tayla's mother is 4 times her age. If Tayla's mother is 48, how old is Tayla?

48 ÷ 4 = 12   **Answer** 12 years old

Elliot read for 80 minutes on Saturday. He read for 5 times as long on Saturday as on Sunday. How long did he read for on Sunday?

80 ÷ 5 = 17   **Answer** 17 minutes

Donna bought a pair of jeans for $45 and a shirt. The jeans cost 5 times as much as the shirt. How much did the shirt cost?

45 ÷ 5 = 9   **Answer** $ 9

Riley saved 5 times as much in March as in April. He saved $85 in March. How much did he save in April?

85 ÷ 5 = 7   **Answer** $ 7

A diner sold 6 times as many pieces of apple pie as cherry pie. The diner sold 78 pieces of apple pie. How many pieces of cherry pie were sold?

78 ÷ 6 = 18   **Answer** 13 pieces

8 The table represents how many pieces of pizza a store sold each day. The store sold 3 times as many pieces of pizza on Sunday than on Monday, and 4 times as many pieces of pizza on Sunday than on Tuesday. Complete the table to show the number of pieces sold on Monday and Tuesday.

Sunday	Monday	Tuesday
▷▷▷▷▷▷ ▷▷▷▷▷▷ ▷▷▷▷▷▷ ▷▷▷▷▷▷ ▷▷▷▷▷▷ ▷▷▷▷▷▷	108	432

9 Lori is packing cans into boxes. She can fit 24 cans in each box. She has 360 cans to pack. Write an equation that can be used to find the total number of boxes she will need. Then solve the equation to find the answer.

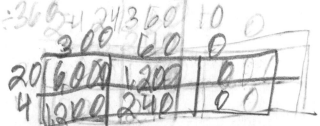

Answer __8,640__ boxes

10 A baker makes 3 times as many plain loaves of bread as multigrain loaves of bread each morning. On Sunday, he made 360 plain loaves of bread. How many loaves of bread did he make in all?

Show your work.

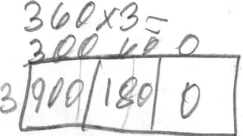

Answer __1,080__ loaves

He sells each loaf of bread for $3. He sold $1,386 worth of the bread he baked on Sunday. How many loaves of bread would be left over?

Show your work.

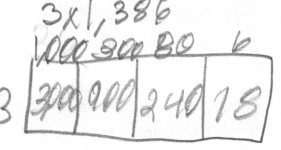

Answer __4,158__ loaves

11 There are 48 students going rafting. Each raft can hold 12 students. If the students are divided evenly, how many rafts will be needed? Show how to find the answer on the number line below. Then write the answer.

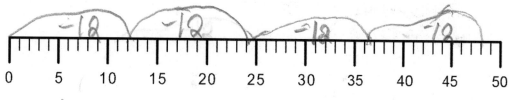

Answer __4__ rafts

Quiz 5: Understanding Remainders

1 Samantha has a packet of 80 candies. She wants to divide them so that each person receives the same number of candies. What is the most number of candies each person can receive?

Ⓐ 8   Ⓑ 9   Ⓒ 10   Ⓓ 12

2 Andrew has 76 photos to place in an album. He can fit 8 photos on each page. If he puts 8 photos on each page and the remainder on the last page, how many photos will be on the last page?

Ⓐ 4   Ⓑ 5   Ⓒ 6   Ⓓ 8

3 The diagram below shows how Jamie divided 18 quarters into groups of 4.

Based on the diagram, what is 18 divided by 4?

Ⓐ 4 r 1   Ⓑ 4 r 2   Ⓒ 5 r 1   Ⓓ 5 r 2

4 Camille has $46. She is buying tickets that cost $8 each. She writes the following equation to model the situation.

$$46 \div 8 = 5 \text{ r } 6$$

Which statement best explains what "5 r 6" in the equation shows?

Ⓐ Camille can buy either 5 or 6 tickets.

Ⓑ Camille can buy 5 tickets and will have $6 left.

Ⓒ Camille can buy 6 tickets and will have $5 left.

Ⓓ Camille can buy 5 lots of 6 tickets.

5   Complete each division calculation below. Write the answer and the remainder on the line.

$42 \div 4 =$ ___10___ r ___2___ $30 \div 7 =$ ___28___ r ___7___

$85 \div 10 =$ ___8___ r ___5___ $33 \div 6 =$ ___6___ r ___3___

$32 \div 3 =$ ___10___ r ___2___ $55 \div 8 =$ ___48___ r ___8___

$27 \div 2 =$ ___13___ r ___1___ $86 \div 9 =$ ___9___ r ___5___

$43 \div 5 =$ ___8___ r ___3___ $68 \div 12 =$ ___5___ r ___8___

6   Julian is planning how to organize 98 runners in the heats of a running race. He can have from 8 to 12 heats. Complete the table to show how many runners will be in each heat and how many runners will be left over.

Number of Runners	Number of Heats	Number of Runners per Heat	Runners Left Over
98	8	12	2
98	9	10	8
98	10	9	8
98	11	9	8
98	12	8	2

Julian decides to have the number of heats with the greatest remainder, and have the remaining runners compete in a last heat. Complete the sentence to describe the heats.

There will be _____ heats with _____ runners, and 1 heat with _____ runners.

7   Lexi has 30 apples. She wants to sort them into groups of 8 apples each. Draw circles around the apples to show the groups.

How many groups of 8 apples are there? __3__ groups

How many apples are left over? __6__ apples

8   Ramona has 28 lettuces to plants. She plants them in rows of 6 lettuces each. Complete the diagram to show how many rows of lettuces she will have and how many will be left over. Then complete the equation that describes the situation.

L L   L   L   L L
L L   L   L   L   L
L L   L   L   L   L
L L   L   L   L   L

Equation __28__ ÷ __6__ = __24__ r __4__

9   Jacinta has 50 flowers to divide evenly between vases. She wants to place 12 flowers in each vase. How many vases can she fill and how many flowers will be left over? Show how to find the answer on the number line below. Then write the answer on the line.

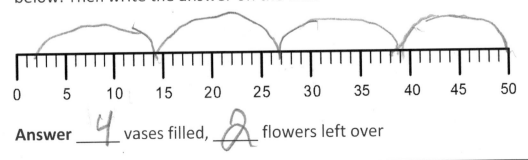

Answer __4__ vases filled, __2__ flowers left over

10 Kieran has 63 books to divide evenly between 6 shelves. Explain why this is not possible.

Cause 6x10=60 r 3.

Describe two ways he could divide the books evenly.

1. 7x9=63

2. 6x10=60

11 Mr. Conrad has 338 flashcards. He wants to give an equal number to 8 groups of students. He writes the expression below.

$$40 + 40 + 40 + 40 + 40 + 40 + 40 + 40 + 18 = 338$$

What does this expression show about how many flashcards each group will get and how many will be left over?

Each group will get 40 and 18 left over

12 Lila has 46 friends to seat at a party. She seats 6 people at each table. She writes the equation below to model the situation.

$$46 \div 6 = 7 \ r \ 4$$

What does "7 r 4" in the equation show about the seating?

That they have 7 tables a 4 friends left.

Quiz 6: Solving Multi-step Problems

1   Jessica and Leroy combined their savings of $32 and $16. They used all their savings to buy movie tickets for $6 each. How many movie tickets did they buy?

   Ⓐ 3   Ⓑ 7   Ⓒ 8   Ⓓ 12

2   Sylvia earns $7 for each car she washes. She washed 14 cars one day, and was also given a tip of $3 and a tip of $5. How much did Sylvia earn in all?

   Ⓐ $29   Ⓑ $98   Ⓒ $106   Ⓓ $133

3   Nelson bought 3 books. Each book cost $14. He also bought 4 movies for $12 each. How much did Nelson spend in all?

   Ⓐ $33   Ⓑ $90   Ⓒ $98   Ⓓ $180

4   Tiffany had $244 in her savings account. After spending $68, she had 4 times as much in her account as Brady. How much does Brady have in his account?

   Ⓐ $44   Ⓑ $51   Ⓒ $61   Ⓓ $78

5   The table shows how many computers a store sold on different days.

	Mon	Tue	Wed	Thurs	Fri
Computers Sold	6	22	14	28	40

Which day sold 2 more than twice what was sold on Monday? __Tue__

Which day sold 4 more than 4 times what was sold on Monday? __Tue__

Which day sold 2 times what was sold on Monday and Wednesday combined? __Fri__

6 An ad break has 4 commercials of 30 seconds each and 1 commercial of 15 seconds. How long is the total ad break?

Show your work.

$$4 \times 30 = 120$$
$$1 \times 15 = +15$$
$$\overline{135}$$

Answer ___135___ seconds

7 A sushi chef makes 24 rolls of sushi. Each roll of sushi is cut into 6 pieces, and 4 pieces are sold on each plate.

$$6 \times 4 = 24$$

How many plates of sushi are made?

Show your work.

Answer ___24___ plates

8 A ferry charges $5 for cars and $8 for trucks. On Monday, the ferry transported 24 trucks and 5 times as many cars as trucks. How much did the ferry make on Monday?

Show your work.

$$24 \times 8 = \qquad 24 \times 5 \qquad 192$$

8	160	32

5	100	20

$$192 + 20 = 212$$

Answer $___212___

9 Oliver has $45 in savings. He plans to save $15 each week. How many weeks will it take for Oliver to have a total of over $100?

Show your work.

$$45$$
$$+15$$
$$60$$
$$+15$$
$$75$$
$$+15$$
$$90$$

$$90$$
$$+15$$
$$105$$

Answer _____4_____ weeks

10 Roxy ran four laps of the track in 65 seconds, 68 seconds, 73 seconds, and 69 seconds. Tori ran four laps of the track in a total time that was 18 seconds less than Roxy's total time. What was Tori's total time?

Show your work.

$$65$$
$$+68$$
$$133$$

$$133$$
$$+73$$
$$206$$

$$206$$
$$+69$$
$$275$$

$$275$$
$$-18$$
$$257$$

Answer __257__ seconds

11 Jacob is buying 4 tires for his car. The price of four brands he can choose from is shown below.

Brand	Dyno	Royal	Hawk	Jetson
Price per tire	$85	$65	$120	$145

Jacob is also charged a total fee of $45 for fitting the four tires. Find the total cost of fitting each brand of tire.

Show your work.

$$120$$
$$+45$$
$$165$$

$$85$$
$$+45$$
$$130$$

$$145$$
$$+45$$
$$190$$

$$65$$
$$+45$$
$$110$$

Dyno $130 **Royal** $110 **Hawk** $165 **Jetson** $190

12 A theater is selling tickets to a play. There will be 4 shows each week and the theater can seat 160 people for each show. The price of tickets to the show is shown below.

Type	Child	Adult	Senior
Price	$7	$12	$10

What is the most that can be made each week if the theater is filled for every show?

Show your work.

$7 \times 12 = 84$
$7 \times 8 = 56$

Answer $ 126

For the Monday show, the theater sold 38 child tickets, 110 adult tickets, and 22 senior tickets. How much was made in all for that show?

Show your work.

Answer $ 1,786

38×7 110×12 22×10

The Thursday show sold 12 child tickets, 75 adult tickets, and 16 senior tickets. The amount made for the Friday show was 3 times the amount made for the Thursday show. How much did the Friday show make?

Show your work.

Answer $ 3,432

Quiz 7: Representing Word Problems with Equations

1   Harley had $84 in his bank account. He took out $30. Then he received $2 in interest. Which expression shows how much he would have in his account now?

Ⓐ $84 + $30 + $2   Ⓑ $84 + $30 − $2

🅒 $84 − $30 + $2   Ⓓ $84 − $30 − $2

2   Jay made 8 trays of 6 muffins each.

He gave 12 muffins away. He packed the remaining muffins in bags of 4 muffins each. Which expression can be used to find how many bags of muffins he packed?

Ⓐ (8 × 6) − 12 ÷ 4   Ⓑ (8 × 6) − (12 ÷ 4)

Ⓒ 8 × (6 − 12 ÷ 4)   🅓 (8 × 6 − 12) ÷ 4

3   Bryant was reading a book with 240 pages. He read 80 pages in the first week. He wants to finish the book in 5 days. Which expression can be used to find how many pages he needs to read each day to finish the book in 5 days?

Ⓐ 240 ÷ 5 − 80   Ⓑ 240 − 80 ÷ 5

Ⓒ 240 − (80 ÷ 5)   🅓 (240 − 80) ÷ 5

4   There were 90 roses planted in a garden. There were 15 roses in each row. Which number sentences could be used to find how rows there were, r? Select all the correct answers.

☐ 90 ÷ r = 15   ☑ 90 ÷ 15 = r

☐ 15 × r = 90   ☐ r × 15 = 90

☐ 15 ÷ r = 90   ☐ 15 × 90 = r

5 Write an equation to match each statement. Use *n* to represent the missing number. Then find the missing number. The first one has been completed for you.

Statement	Equation	Missing Number
16 more than a number is equal to 44	$n + 16 = 44$	28
a number times 12 is equal to 72	$12 \times n = 72$	6
25 less than a number is equal to 68	$n - 25 = 68$	93
88 divided by a number is equal to 4	$88 \div 4 = n$	22
the sum of a number and 54 is equal to 89		
a number divided by 3 is equal to 27	$3 \times n = 27$	7
7 times as many as a number is equal to 140		
a number is 9 times as many as 14		

6 A store sells sandwiches for $6 each. Complete the equation that can be used to solve each problem.

How many sandwiches, *s*, can be bought for $30? $30 \div 6 = 5$

What will be the total cost, *t*, of buying 8 sandwiches? $6 \times 8 = 48$

How much change, *c*, should a person get when paying for 3 sandwiches with $20? $(6 \times 3) + 2 = 20$

7 Malcolm paid a flat fee of $25 to hire a bike, plus a fee of $10 per hour. Write the correct symbols in the expression to show how to find the total cost, c, of hiring a bike for 4 hours.

$$25 \boxed{-} 10 \boxed{+} 4 = c$$

8 Max has 4 fish. He feeds each fish 5 food pellets per day. Each jar of fish food has 300 pellets in it. Complete the equation to show how many days, d, one jar of fish food lasts. Then solve the equation to find the answer.

$$(\underline{4} \times \underline{5}) \times d = \underline{320}$$

Answer __320__ days

9 Samuel wants to finish a hike in 60 minutes. He finished the first section in 17 minutes and the second section in 19 minutes. Complete the equation to show how many minutes, m, he must finish the final section in to reach his goal. Then solve the equation to find the answer.

$$\underline{36} + \underline{24} + m = \underline{60}$$

$$\begin{array}{r} 17 \\ + 19 \\ \hline 36 \end{array}$$

Answer __24__ minutes

10 Jin has $40 to spend on school supplies. He bought 2 folders for $6 each and 4 pens for $4 each. He is going to spend the remaining amount on notebooks for $2 each. Complete the equation to show how many notebooks, n, he can buy. Then solve the equation to find the answer.

$$(\underline{\quad} \times \underline{\quad}) + (\underline{\quad} \times \underline{\quad}) + (\underline{\quad} \times n) = 40$$

Answer _____ notebooks

11 Becky counted 3 rainy days in March. She counted 2 times as many rainy days in April as in March. Write an equation to find the number of rainy days, *r*, in March and April. Then solve the equation to find the answer.

$3 \times 2 = 6$

Answer _____6_____ rainy days

12 The table below shows the pizzas a store sold one day. Small pizzas sell for $9 each and large pizzas sell for $14 each.

Type	Small Pizzas Sold	Large Pizzas Sold
Pepperoni	18	22
Supreme	24	35
Vegetarian	15	12
Chicken	c	30

Write an equation to show the number of dollars made, *d*, from the sale of pepperoni pizzas. Then solve the equation to find the answer.

Answer $_____308_____

Write an equation to show how many more supreme pizzas, *s*, were sold than vegetarian pizzas. Then solve the equation to find the answer.

Answer _____38_____ pizzas

The store made $600 from the sale of chicken pizzas. Write an equation to show the number of small chicken pizzas sold, *c*. Then solve the equation to find the answer.

Answer _____179_____ pizzas

Quiz 8: Using Estimation and Rounding

1 Which is the best way to estimate the product of 28 and 44?

Ⓐ 20 × 40   Ⓑ 20 × 50   Ⓒ 30 × 40   Ⓓ 30 × 50

2 Five friends are dividing a bill of $63 evenly. Which is the closest estimate of how much each friend will pay?

Ⓐ $12   Ⓑ $13   Ⓒ $14   Ⓓ $15

3 Which is the best estimate of how much greater the population of Milton is than Mayfair?

Town	Population
Mayfair	17,901
Milton	22,182
Lexington	27,855

Ⓐ 4,000   Ⓑ 5,000   Ⓒ 9,000   Ⓓ 10,000

4 The list shows how many cans each class collected for a food drive.

Miss Adams 68, Mr. Walsh 52, Mrs. Naroda 37

Which is the best estimate of the number of cans collected in all?

Ⓐ 140   Ⓑ 150   Ⓒ 160   Ⓓ 170

5 The table lists the ages of five family members.

Name	Ben	Ann	Leah	Toby	Roy
Age	11	16	23	37	7

Which two have a combined age closest to 40? ___ and ___

Who is closest to being 3 times Ben's age? ___

Who is closest to being 4 times Roy's age? ___

6 Tara worked for 42 hours and earned $18 per hour. Which is the best estimate of the total amount she made?

Ⓐ $400   Ⓑ $600   Ⓒ $800   Ⓓ $900

7 A mail carrier delivered 2,482 letters in the morning and 578 letters in the afternoon. Which is the best estimate of the number of letters delivered in all?

Ⓐ 2,500   Ⓑ 2,600   Ⓒ 2,900   Ⓓ 3,100

8 A train travels 68 miles in 1 hour. If the train travels at the same speed, which is the best way to estimate how many miles the train travels in 4 hours?

Ⓐ 70 × 4 = 280   Ⓑ 65 × 4 = 260   Ⓒ 70 × 5 = 350   Ⓓ 60 × 5 = 300

9 Round the two-digit number down and up to the nearest ten to find two numbers the product will be between. Then complete the sentence.

81 × 6   ____ × 6 = ____   ____ × 6 = ____

The product of 81 and 6 will be between ____ and ____.

47 × 5   ____ × 5 = ____   ____ × 5 = ____

The product of 47 and 5 will be between ____ and ____.

93 × 7   ____ × 7 = ____   ____ × 7 = ____

The product of 93 and 7 will be between ____ and ____.

72 × 9   ____ × 9 = ____   ____ × 9 = ____

The product of 72 and 9 will be between ____ and ____.

38 × 8   ____ × 8 = ____   ____ × 8 = ____

The product of 38 and 8 will be between ____ and ____.

10   Estimate each division problem by completing the division of the nearest number lower and higher that divides evenly. Then complete the sentence. The first one has been completed for you.

$48 \div 5$ $45 \div 5 = 9$ $50 \div 5 = 10$

The result of $48 \div 5$ will be between 9 and 10.

$26 \div 5$ $26 \div 5 = 4 R1$ $30 \div 5 = 6$

The result of $26 \div 5$ will be between __4__ and __6__.

$33 \div 4$ $32 \div 4 = 8 R1$ $30 \div 4 = 7 R2$

The result of $33 \div 4$ will be between __7__ and __8__.

$40 \div 6$ $40 \div 6 = 36 R4$ $40 \div 6 = 36 R4$

The result of $40 \div 6$ will be between __36__ and __36__.

$83 \div 8$ $83 \div 8 = 10 R3$ $80 \div 8 = 10$

The result of $83 \div 8$ will be between __10__ and __10__.

11   Victor sent a total of 96 text messages in 31 days. About how many text messages did he send each day?

Show your work.

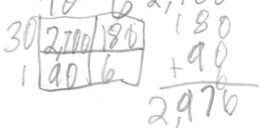

Answer __3,000__ messages

12   An online bookstore sells 48 books every hour. At this rate, about how many books will the bookstore sell in 8 hours?

Show your work.

Answer __380__ books

13 Cans of chicken soup are sold in boxes of 24. A grocery store ordered 205 boxes of chicken soup. Round each number to the nearest ten to estimate how many cans of chicken soup the store ordered.

Show your work.

200
·20
20

Answer *220* cans

Is your estimate less than or greater than the actual amount ordered? Explain your answer.

My answer is less than because my answer is 220 and there is 224.

14 Parker wants to order 67 hats for the members of the science club. He has $300 to spend on hats. He completes the estimation below.

$$300 \div 60 = 5$$

He states that he can buy all the hats he needs if the hats are $5 each. Explain what is wrong with Parker's decision.

He wants to buy 67 and his equation says 300÷60=5.

15 Molly saved $7 each week for 38 weeks. Would she have saved just under $280 or just over $280? Explain your answer.

30 8
7 40 56

She saved under because the answer is 266.

Quiz 9: Understanding and Using Factors

1   Which number is a factor of 57?

   Ⓐ 11   Ⓑ 13   Ⓒ 17   Ⓓ 19

2   What are all the factors of 8?

   Ⓐ 1, 8   Ⓑ 2, 4   Ⓒ 1, 4, 8   Ⓓ 1, 2, 4, 8

3   What are all the common factors of 8, 24, and 60?

   Ⓐ 1, 2, 4   Ⓑ 1, 2, 4, 8   Ⓒ 1, 2, 4, 6   Ⓓ 1, 2, 4, 6, 8

4   A play sold $98 worth of tickets. Each ticket cost the same amount.

Which of these could be the cost of each ticket?

   Ⓐ $6   Ⓑ $8   Ⓒ $12   Ⓓ $14

5   What factors do 18, 24, and 36 have in common? Select all the correct answers.

   ☐ 2   ☐ 3   ☐ 4   ☐ 6

   ☐ 8   ☐ 9   ☐ 12   ☐ 18

6   Janelle divided 76 coins into equal piles. Which of these could be the number of coins in each pile? Select all the possible answers.

   ☐ 2   ☐ 3   ☐ 4   ☐ 5

   ☐ 6   ☐ 7   ☐ 8   ☐ 9

   ☐ 11   ☐ 13   ☐ 17   ☐ 19

7   Write multiplication expressions to complete the list of all the factors pairs for each number.

Number	Factor Pairs			
28	1 × 28	2 × 14	7 × 4	
44	1 × 44	11 × 4	4 × 11	
50	1 × 50	25 × 2	10 × 5	
63	1 × 63	7 × 9	9 × 7	
66	1 × 66	11 × 6	6 × ___	___ × ___
78	1 × 78	12 × 6	___ × ___	___ × ___
88	1 × 88	11 × 8	___ × ___	___ × ___

8   The table below shows how much the staff of a restaurant made on Friday. Each person worked a whole number of hours, and each wage is a whole number amount from $5 to $15. For each person, list the possible amounts they could make per hour.

Name	Total Wages ($)	Possible Hourly Amounts ($)
Bruce	55	____ or ____
Emmett	65	____ or ____
Didi	48	____ or ____ or ____
Gwen	42	____ or ____ or ____
Donnie	56	____ or ____ or ____
Bianca	72	____ or ____ or ____ or ____

9 List all the factors of each number below.

28 4, 7, 1, 2, 14, and 28

35 7, 5, 1, and 35

70 10, 7, 1, 70, 5, 14, 2, and 35

Which numbers are common factors of 28, 35, and 70? __7__ and __1__

10 One factor of each number is listed below. Write and solve a division equation to find the other number in the factor pair. The first one has been completed for you.

Number	First Factor	Division Equation	Factor Pair
20	4	$20 \div 4 = 5$	4 and 5
75	3	$70 \div 3 = 25$	3 and 25
96	6	$96 \div 6 = 16$	6 and 16
76	4	$76 \div 4 = 19$	4, 19
98	14	$98 \div 14 = 7$	14, 7
84	21	$84 \div 21 = 3$	21, 3

11 Complete the statement to describe what the number line below shows.

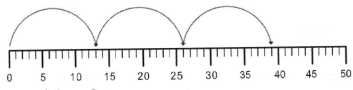

A factor pair of __13__ is __26__ and __39__.

12 Use the number line below to show that 15 is a factor of 90. Then use the number line you completed to complete the factor pair.

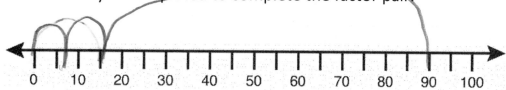

Factor pair _6_ **and 15**

Use the number line below to find one other factor pair of 90.

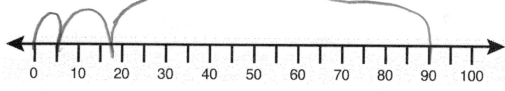

Factor pair _5_ **and** _18_

13 Hannah shaded the grid to show two ways 45 squares can be arranged into a rectangle. Use the diagram to complete the list of the factors of 45.

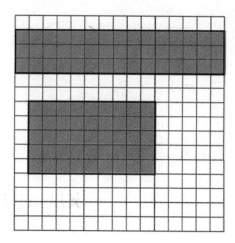

The factors of 45 are 1, 45, _5_ , _9_ , _3_ , and _15_ .

On the lines below, explain how the rectangles show the factors of 45.

It helps me on how
they are reanged.

Quiz 10: Understanding and Using Multiples

1   Which number is a multiple of 6?

    Ⓐ 3   Ⓑ 20   Ⓒ 36   Ⓓ 50

2   Which number is a multiple of 14?

    Ⓐ 2   Ⓑ 7   Ⓒ 42   Ⓓ 80

3   Which number is a factor of 36 and a multiple of 9?

    Ⓐ 3   Ⓑ 6   Ⓒ 12   Ⓓ 18

4   A farmer sells eggs in cartons of 6 eggs each.

    A bakery placed an order for several cartons of 6 eggs. Which of these could be the total number of eggs ordered?

    Ⓐ 48   Ⓑ 50   Ⓒ 52   Ⓓ 56

5   Leticia used muffin tins like the one below to bake batches of muffins for a bake sale. The muffin tin was full for each batch.

    Which of these could be the total number of muffins she baked? Select all the possible answers.

    ☐ 18   ☑ 24   ☐ 30   ☐ 42

    ☑ 48   ☐ 52   ☑ 60   ☐ 84

6   Which factors of 60 are also multiples of 5? Select all the correct answers.

    ☑ 1   ☐ 2   ☐ 3   ☐ 4

    ☑ 5   ☑ 6   ☑ 10   ☑ 12

    ☑ 15   ☑ 20   ☑ 30   ☑ 60

7   Complete the list of all the multiples of each number from 0 to 100.

Number	Multiples
10	10, *20, 30, 40, 50, 60, 70, 80, 90, 100*
11	11, *22, 33, 44, 55, 66, 77, 88, 99*
12	12, *24, 36, 48, 60, 72, 84, 96*
14	14, *28, 42, 56, 70, 84, 98*
15	15, *30, 45, 60, 75, 90*
18	18, *32, 50, 68, 86*
20	20, *40, 60, 80, 100*

8   Complete the list of all the multiples from 0 to 50 of each number below.

4   4, *8, 12, 16, 20, 24, 28, 32, 36, 40, 44, 48*

6   6, *12, 18, 24, 30, 36, 42, 48*

8   8, *16, 24, 32, 40, 48*

Which numbers are multiples of 4 and 6? *24, 36, 12*, and *48*

Which numbers are multiples of 4, 6, and 8? *24* and *48*

9   Kelly drew a 13 by 8 rectangle on a grid and shaded each row of the rectangle. Complete the statements about the rectangle below. Then complete the list of the first 8 multiples of 13.

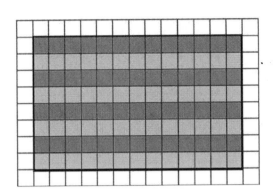

There are ___13___ squares in 1 row.   There are ___65___ squares in 5 rows.

There are ___26___ squares in 2 rows.   There are ___78___ squares in 6 rows.

There are ___39___ squares in 3 rows.   There are ___91___ squares in 7 rows.

There are ___52___ squares in 4 rows.   There are ___104___ squares in 8 rows.

The first 8 multiples of 13 are __13__, __26__, __39__, __52__, __65__, __78__, __91__, and __104__.

10   Draw a 17 by 5 rectangle on the grid below. Use the rectangle to find the first 5 multiples of 17.

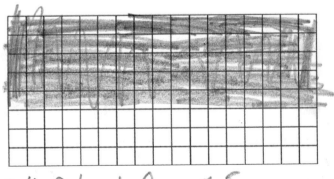

Answer __17__, __34__, __51__, __68__, and __85__

11 Based on the number line below, what are the first 3 multiples of 16?

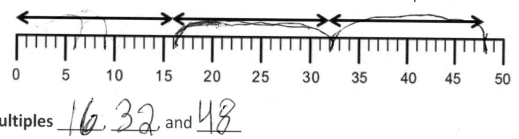

Multiples _16, 32_, and _48_

12 Use the number line below to show all the multiples of 9 from 0 to 50. List the multiples below.

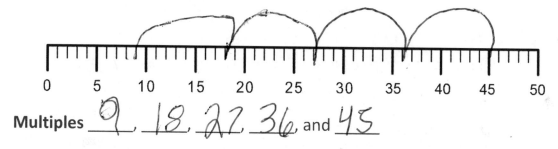

Multiples _9, 18, 27, 36_, and _45_

13 Stuart makes the first layer of a wall by placing 6 bricks in a row. He uses another 6 bricks to make the second row. He keeps adding layers of 6 bricks until the wall is complete.

Which of these could be the total number of bricks in the wall? Circle all the possible answers.

22 (24) 32 (36) 40 44 (48) 52 58 64

Explain why the numbers you did not circle are not possible answers.

The others are not a multiple of 6.

Quiz 11: Identifying Prime and Composite Numbers

1   Which statement best proves that 29 is a prime number?

 Ⓐ It can be divided by 1.

 Ⓑ It is an odd number.

 Ⓒ It cannot be evenly divided by 3.

 Ⓓ It can only be divided evenly by 29 and 1.

2   Jordan states that the number 57 is a prime number. Which statement best explains how you can tell that Jordan is incorrect?

 Ⓐ The number 57 is an odd number.

 Ⓑ The number 57 is a two-digit number.

 Ⓒ The number 57 can be evenly divided by 3.

 Ⓓ The number 57 is made up of 5 tens and 7 ones.

3   Which number sentence proves that 35 is a composite number?

 Ⓐ $35 \times 1 = 35$ Ⓑ $35 \div 5 = 7$ Ⓒ $35 \times 2 = 70$ Ⓓ $35 \div 10 = 3\ r\ 5$

4   Which number is a prime number?

 Ⓐ 93   Ⓑ 95   Ⓒ 97   Ⓓ 99

5   Which number is a composite number?

 Ⓐ 41   Ⓑ 43   Ⓒ 47   Ⓓ 49

6   Which numbers are prime numbers? Select all the correct answers.

 ☐ 31   ☐ 33   ☐ 34   ☐ 37

 ☐ 51   ☐ 53   ☐ 57   ☐ 59

7 Four students used blocks to make rectangles, as shown below.

Student	Dimensions	Rectangle
April	5 by 1	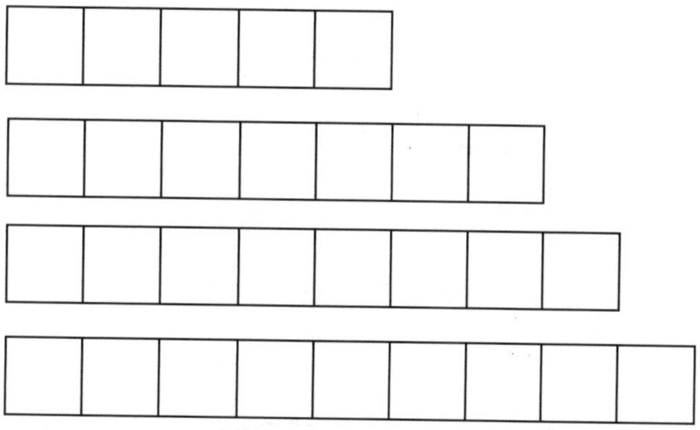
Kacey	7 by 1	
Joya	8 by 1	
Mona	9 by 1	

Which two students could use all the blocks to make a rectangle with different dimensions? _Joya_ and _Mona_

What does this tell you about whether the numbers 5, 7, 8, and 9 are prime or composite? Explain your answer.

This is composite 8, 9 and this is prime 5, 7.

8 How can you tell that all the numbers listed are composite numbers?

15, 25, 35, 45, 55, 65, 75, 85, 95

You can divide them more than once.

9 Lauren states that every even number greater than 2 is a composite number. Is Lauren correct? Explain why or why not.

No because they can't be divided more than once.

Quiz 12: Generating Patterns

1 Which procedure can be used to find the next number in the pattern?

240, 120, 60, 30, …

Ⓐ Subtract 15 from the previous number

Ⓑ Add 15 to the previous number

Ⓒ Multiply the previous number by 2

Ⓓ Divide the previous number by 2

2 Which number comes next in the pattern below?

4, 12, 20, 28, 36, …

Ⓐ 30   Ⓑ 44   Ⓒ 48   Ⓓ 64

3 Which number comes next in the pattern below?

85, 77, 69, 61, 53, …

Ⓐ 32   Ⓑ 37   Ⓒ 45   Ⓓ 48

4 A pattern starts at 9 and follows the rule "Add 5." What is the third number in the pattern?

Ⓐ 14   Ⓑ 15   Ⓒ 19   Ⓓ 24

5 A pattern is shown below.

8, 16, 24, 32, 40, 48, …

Select all the numbers that could be in the pattern.

☐ 62   ☐ 64   ☐ 70   ☐ 72

☐ 78   ☐ 84   ☐ 96   ☐ 98

6 Complete the first 6 terms of each pattern described below.

starts at 5, adds 4 to each number

5 , 9 , 13 , 17 , 21 , 26

starts at 80, subtracts 3 from each number

80 , 77 , 74 , 71 , 68 , 65

starts at 2, each number is twice the one before it

2 , 4 , 8 , 16 , 32 , 64

starts at 5, adds 7 to each number

5 , 12 , 19 , 26 , 33 , 40

starts at 35, each number is 6 less than the one before it

35 , 29 , 23 , 17 , 11 , 5

starts at 16, adds 9 to each number

16 , 25 , 34 , 43 , 52 , 61

starts at 1, each number is 3 times the one before it

1 , 4 , 12 , 24 , 48 , 96

starts at 10, each number is 8 more than the one before it

10 , 18 , 26 , 34 , 42 , 50

starts at 3, each number is twice the one before it

3 , 6 , 12 , 24 , 48 , 96

starts at 4, multiplies each number by 10

4 , 40 , 400 , 4,000 , 40,000 , 400,000

7 Henry has $280 in savings. He spends $16 each week for 6 weeks. Complete the pattern that shows how much Henry has left, in dollars, at the end of each week.

280, *264*, *248*, *232*, *216*, *200*, *184*

8 The perimeter of a square is always 4 times the side length of the square. Complete the table with the perimeter of each square.

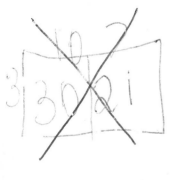

Side length (cm)	Perimeter (cm)
2	*8*
3	*12*
4	*16*
5	*20*
6	*24*

9 There are 3 feet in 1 yard. Complete the table with the missing measurements.

Length in Yards	Length in Feet
6	*18*
9	27
14	42
17	*51*
21	*63*
26	78

10 Georgia drew the first 3 terms of a shape pattern, as shown below. Draw the fourth term of the shape pattern.

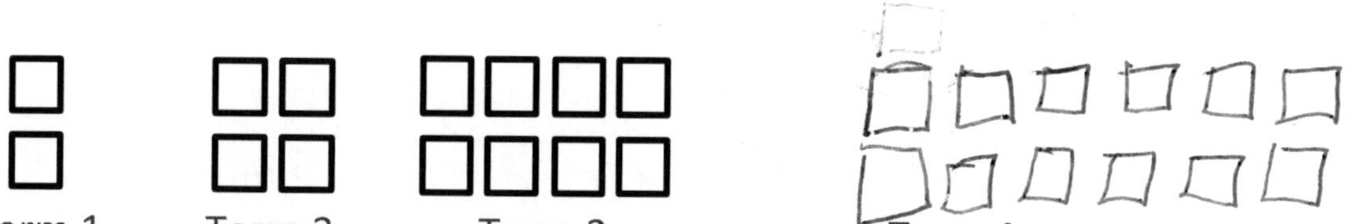

Term 1   Term 2   Term 3   Term 4

Complete the rule for the pattern Georgia made.

The pattern starts with _2_ squares. Each term has _2_ times as many squares as the one before it.

11 Kennedy sorted marbles into groups in a set pattern. The first three sets of her pattern are shown below. Draw Set 4 and Set 5 of the pattern.

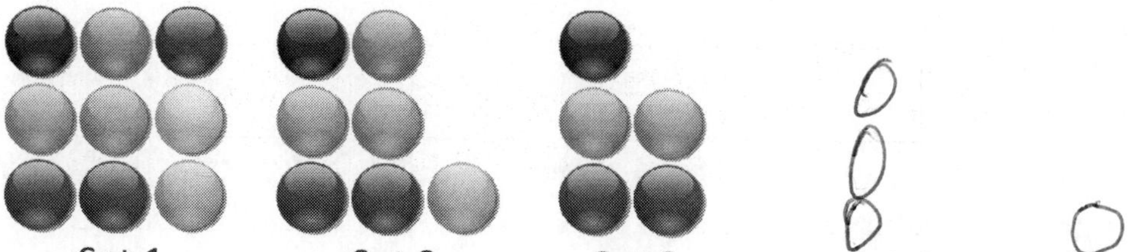

Set 1   Set 2   Set 3   Set 4   Set 5

Describe the rule for the pattern Kennedy made.

To remove 2 every time.

12 Levi writes the pattern below.

5, 10, 15, 20, 25, 30, 35, 40, 45, 50, ...

If Levi continues the pattern until he reaches 200, will the number 185 be a number in the pattern? Explain how you can tell.

It will because he's skipping 5.

Quiz 13: Describing and Analyzing Patterns

1   The table shows the total number of beads Simone uses to make different numbers of bracelets.

Number of Bracelets	Number of Beads
3	18
4	24
5	30

Which of the following describes the relationship in the table?

Ⓐ number of bracelets + 15 = number of beads

Ⓑ number of bracelets + 25 = number of beads

Ⓒ number of bracelets × 6 = number of beads

Ⓓ number of bracelets × 8 = number of beads

2   If n is a number in the pattern, which rule can be used to find the next number in the pattern?

$$38, 34, 30, 26, 22, 18, 14, 10, 6, 2, \dots$$

Ⓐ $n + 2$ Ⓑ $n - 2$ Ⓒ $n + 4$ Ⓓ $n - 4$

3   The table below shows the total number of chairs that are needed to go with different numbers of tables.

Number of Tables	Number of Chairs
4	24
6	36
10	60

How many chairs would be needed for 12 tables?

Ⓐ 48   Ⓑ 62   Ⓒ 72   Ⓓ 96

4 The first six numbers in a pattern are shown below. Which statement is true about every number in the pattern?

15, 30, 45, 60, 75, 90, ...

Ⓐ It is a multiple of 15.   Ⓑ It is divisible by 10.

Ⓒ It is a factor of 90.   Ⓓ It is an even number.

5 A camp has 1 adult for a set number of students. The table below shows the relationship between the number of adults at the camp and the number of students at the camp.

Number of Adults	5	7	10	13	16	19
Number of Students	60	84	120	156	192	216

Write equations that can be solved to find the number of students when there are 10 and 13 adults. Write the missing numbers in the table.

$$10 \times 12 = 120 \qquad 13 \times 12 = 156$$

Write equations that can be solved to find the number of adults when there are 192 and 216 students. Write the missing numbers in the table.

$$16 \times 12 = 192 \qquad 19 \times 12 = 216$$

6 Leila starts two different patterns with the numbers 2 and 4, as shown below. Use a different rule to complete each pattern. Write the rule you used next to the pattern.

Pattern	Rule
2, 4, 8, 16, 32, 64, 128, 256	× 2
2, 4, 6, 8, 10, 12, 14, 16	+ 2

7 For each pattern, write an expression that can be used to find the next number in the pattern. Use *n* to represent the last number in the pattern. Then complete the missing numbers.

Pattern			**Expression**
2, 5, 8, 11, 14, 17,	20	23	+ 3
3, 6, 12, 24, 48,	96	192	× 2
40, 36, 32, 28, 24,	20	16	− 4
1, 6, 11, 16, 21, 26,	31	36	+ 5
100, 89, 78, 67, 56,	45	34	− 11
1, 4, 16, 64, 256,	1,024	4,096	× 4

8 Complete each pattern described below.

The first number is 8. The pattern follows the rule "Add 12."

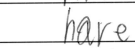

8, 20, 32, 44, 56, 68

The first number is 75. The pattern follows the rule "Subtract 6."

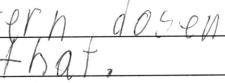

75, 69, 63, 57, 51, 45

Explain why the first pattern only has even numbers and why the second pattern only has odd numbers.

The pattern dosen't have that.

9   Vanessa has a rectangular notecard with an area of 192 square centimeters. She cuts it in half. She then cuts the half in half again. She continues this for a total of 6 times.

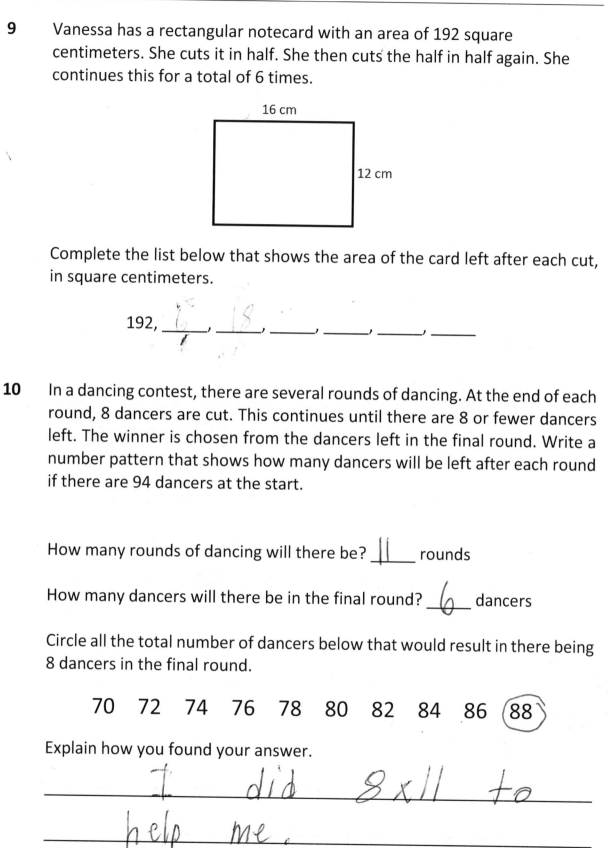

16 cm

12 cm

Complete the list below that shows the area of the card left after each cut, in square centimeters.

192, __6__, __18__, _____, _____, _____, _____

10   In a dancing contest, there are several rounds of dancing. At the end of each round, 8 dancers are cut. This continues until there are 8 or fewer dancers left. The winner is chosen from the dancers left in the final round. Write a number pattern that shows how many dancers will be left after each round if there are 94 dancers at the start.

How many rounds of dancing will there be? __11__ rounds

How many dancers will there be in the final round? __6__ dancers

Circle all the total number of dancers below that would result in there being 8 dancers in the final round.

70   72   74   76   78   80   82   84   86   (88)

Explain how you found your answer.

_____I___ did ___8×11___ to_____

____help___me._____

Quizzes 14 to 23

Number and Operations in Base Ten

Directions

Read each question carefully. For each multiple-choice question, fill in the circle for the correct answer. For other types of questions, follow the directions given in the question.

You may use a ruler to help you answer questions. You should answer the questions without using a calculator.

MATHEMATICS SKILLS LIST
For Parents, Teachers, and Tutors

Quizzes 14 through 23 cover these skills from the Georgia Standards of Excellence.

Number and Operations in Base Ten

Generalize place value understanding for multi-digit whole numbers.

1. Recognize that in a multi-digit whole number, a digit in one place represents ten times what it represents in the place to its right.

2. Read and write multi-digit whole numbers using base-ten numerals, number names, and expanded form. Compare two multi-digit numbers based on meanings of the digits in each place, using >, =, and < symbols to record the results of comparisons.

3. Use place value understanding to round multi-digit whole numbers to any place.

Use place value understanding and properties of operations to perform multi-digit arithmetic.

4. Fluently add and subtract multi-digit whole numbers using the standard algorithm.

5. Multiply a whole number of up to four digits by a one-digit whole number, and multiply two two-digit numbers, using strategies based on place value and the properties of operations. Illustrate and explain the calculation by using equations, rectangular arrays, and/or area models.

6. Find whole-number quotients and remainders with up to four-digit dividends and one-digit divisors, using strategies based on place value, the properties of operations, and/or the relationship between multiplication and division. Illustrate and explain the calculation by using equations, rectangular arrays, and/or area models.

Quiz 14: Understanding Place Value

1   How many times greater is 48,000 than 48?

   Ⓐ 10   Ⓑ 100   Ⓒ 1,000   ⦿ 10,000

2   Which number has a 6 that represents a value ten times greater than the value represented by the 6 in 43,659?

   Ⓐ 62,974   ⦿ 36,072   Ⓒ 28,165   Ⓓ 75,356

3   In the number 787,421 how much greater is the value represented by the 7 in the hundred thousands place than the value represented by the 7 in the thousands place?

   Ⓐ 1   Ⓑ 10   ⦿ 100   Ⓓ 1,000

4   In the number below, how many times greater is the number represented by the digit in the thousands place than the number represented by the digit in the hundreds place?

$$5,265,579$$

   Ⓐ 1   ⦿ 10   Ⓒ 100   Ⓓ 1,000

5   Which pair of numbers correctly completes the equation?

$$_____ \times 100 = _____$$

   Ⓐ 62 and 62,000   Ⓑ 620 and 6,200

   Ⓒ 62 and 620   ⦿ 620 and 62,000

6   What is the value of the expression below?

$$2,800,000 \div 28,000$$

   Ⓐ 1   Ⓑ 10   Ⓒ 100   ⦿ 1,000

7 In which pairs of numbers does the 9 in the first number represent a value 10 times greater than the 9 in the second number? Select all the correct answers.

☐ 900 and 965   ☐ 903 and 96

☐ 9,860 and 2,095   ☐ 3,947 and 6,589

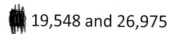 19,548 and 26,975   ☒ 25,982 and 37,590

8 In which of these does a missing number of 100 make the equation true? Select all the correct answers.

☐ 42 × _____ = 4,020   ☐ 4,205 × _____ = 42,500

☒ 68 × _____ = 6,800   ☒ 8,963 × _____ = 896,300

☐ 745 × _____ = 70,045   ☐ 10,008 × _____ = 1,000,008

☐ 309 × _____ = 309,000   ☐ 55,045 × _____ = 55,045,000

9 Complete the table below with the missing numbers.

Number	Number × 10	Number × 100	Number × 1000
85	850	8,500	85,000
751	7,510	75,100	
642	6,420	64,200	642,000
95	950	9,500	95,000
346	3,460	34,600	346,000
2,058	20,580	205,800	2,058,000
673	6,730	67,300	673,000

10 For each pair of numbers, list how much greater the value of the 5 is in the first number than the second.

357	395	10x _____ times greater
3,658	2,905	10 _____ times greater
5,361	2,453	100 _____ times greater
35,008	39,005	1,000 _____ times greater
56,119	96,503	100 _____ times greater
235,622	289,544	10 _____ times greater
590,001	950,001	10 _____ times greater
5,634,000	9,358,000	100 _____ times greater
3,569,074	3,408,257	100,000 _____ times greater

11 Write the missing number on the line to make each equation correct. Then write a multiplication equation that shows that the equation is correct.

$800 \div \underline{10} = 80$ $\underline{10} \times \underline{80} = \underline{800}$

$700 \div \underline{100} = 7$ $\underline{7} \times \underline{100} = \underline{700}$

$3,500 \div \underline{100} = 35$ $\underline{100} \times \underline{35} = \underline{3,500}$

$26,000 \div \underline{1,000} = 26$ $\underline{26} \times \underline{1,000} = \underline{26,000}$

$38,000 \div \underline{1,000} = 380$ $\underline{380} \times \underline{1,000} = \underline{38,000}$

12 Craig is putting pennies into piles of 100. Craig makes 25 piles of 100 pennies. How many pennies does Craig have in all?

Show your work.

$25 \times 100 = 2500$

Answer _2,500_ pennies

13 A box of nails contains 1,000 nails. Maxwell buys 14 boxes of nails. How many nails did Maxwell buy?

Show your work.

$1,000 \times 14 = 14,000$

Answer _14,000_ nails

14 A warehouse manager ordered 28 pairs of work boots for the same cost each. The total order cost $2,800. What was the cost of each pair of work boots?

Show your work.

$2,800 \div 28 = 100$

Answer $_100_

15 Yuri completes the calculation below.

$$600,000 \div 60,000 = 10$$

Explain how place value shows that the calculation is correct.

_____Be cause one is 600,000,_____

60,000

Quiz 15: Reading and Writing Whole Numbers

1   Which phrase represents the number 8,070?

    Ⓐ eighty-seven hundred

    Ⓑ eighty and seventy

    Ⓒ eight thousand and seven

    Ⓓ eight thousand and seventy

2   Which of these shows the number 28,097 in expanded form?

    Ⓐ 280 + 97

    Ⓑ 28,000 + 9 + 7

    Ⓒ 20,000 + 800 + 90 + 7

    Ⓓ 20,000 + 8,000 + 90 + 7

3   An airline employs 10,208 people. Add the missing number to show another way to write 10,208.

$$10,000 + \underline{} + 8$$

4   Which number is represented by the place-value blocks below?

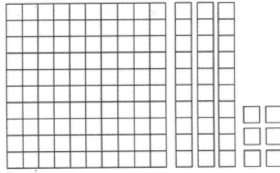

Answer 1036

5 Which of these are ways of writing the number 2,850? Select all the correct answers.

☒ 2,000 + 800 + 5   ☒ 2,800 + 50

☒ (28 × 100) + (5 × 10)   ☒ 2 thousands + 85 tens

☐ two thousand and eighty-five   ☐ 2 thousands + 8 tens + 5 ones

6 Which of the following is another way to write the numeral 6,300,025?

Ⓐ six million, three hundred thousand, twenty-five

Ⓑ six hundred thousand, three hundred and twenty-five

Ⓒ six million, three hundred and twenty-five

Ⓓ six thousand, three hundred, twenty-five

7 Write each number described in words in number form.

twenty thousand and five	20,005
twenty thousand and fifty	20,050
twenty thousand five hundred	20,500
twenty-five thousand	25,000
eight hundred thousand nine hundred	800,900
eight hundred and ninety thousand	890,000
eight hundred thousand and nine	800,009
eight hundred and nine thousand	809,000
eight hundred thousand and ninety	800,090

8 Write numbers on the lines to show each number in expanded form.

435   (_400_ × 100) + (_30_ × 10) + (_5_ × 1)

729   (_700_ × 100) + (_20_ × 10) + (_9_ × 1)

680   (_600_× 100) + (_80_× 10) + (_0_ × 1)

2,517   (_2000_× 1,000) + (_500_× 100) + (_10_ × 10) + (_7_ × 1)

6,359   (_6000_× 1,000) + (_300_× 100) + (_50_ × 10) + (_9_ × 1)

36,509   (_30000_× 10,000) + (_6,000_× 1,000) + (_500_× 100) + (_9_× 1)

28,730   (_20000_×10,000) + (_8,000_×1,000) + (_700_× 100) + (_30_ × 10)

40,562   (_40,000_× 10,000) + (_500_× 100) + (_60_ × 10) + (_2_ × 1)

9 Write each number represented below on the line.

5 × 1,000 + 7 × 100 + 2 × 10 + 6 × 1   _5,726_

3 × 10,000 + 6 × 1,000 + 8 × 100 + 5 × 10 + 9 × 1   _36,859_

6 × 10,000 + 9 × 1,000 + 3 × 10 + 5 × 1   _69,035_

4 × 100,000 + 1 × 10,000 + 3 × 100 + 7 × 1   _4,137_

2 × 100,000 + 7 × 10,000 + 6 × 1,000 + 3 × 10   _276,030_

9 × 100,000 + 8 × 1,000 + 5 × 100 + 2 × 10 + 4 × 1   _908,524_

1 × 1,000,000 + 4 × 100 + 6 × 10 + 7 × 1   _100,000,467_

7 × 1,000,000 + 5 × 100,000 + 9 × 1,000 + 6 × 1 _700,509,006_

10 Complete the blank spaces to show four different ways to represent the number 85,723.

___8___ ten-thousands, ___5___ thousands, ___7___ hundreds, ___2___ tens, ___3___ ones

___5___ ten-thousands, ___7___ thousands, ___2___ hundreds, ___3___ ones

___8___ thousands, ___7___ hundreds, ___2___ tens, ___3___ ones

___7___ thousands, ___2___ tens, ___3___ ones

11 Victoria wrote the three numbers below on the board.

900,000   50,000   4,000

How many hundreds are in 900,000? ___0___ hundreds

How many thousands are in 900,000? ___0___ thousands

How many hundreds are in 50,000? ___0___ hundreds

How many thousands are in 50,000? ___0___ thousands

How many tens are in 4,000? ___0___ tens

How many thousands are in 4,000? ___4___ thousands

Use your answers to complete the equations below.

$900{,}000 = \underline{9000} \times 100$ $900{,}000 = \underline{900} \times 1{,}000$

$50{,}000 = \underline{500} \times 100$ $50{,}000 = \underline{50} \times 1{,}000$

$4{,}000 = \underline{400} \times 10$ $4{,}000 = \underline{4} \times 1{,}000$

Quiz 16: Comparing Whole Numbers

1 Which number is between 6,246 and 6,451?

    Ⓐ 6,512   Ⓑ 6,087   Ⓒ 6,392   Ⓓ 6,460

2 Which number is less than the number below?

    6 thousands + 4 hundreds + 7 tens

    Ⓐ 6 thousands + 7 hundreds + 2 tens

    Ⓑ 6 thousands + 3 hundreds + 5 tens

    Ⓒ 7 thousands + 2 hundreds + 3 tens

    Ⓓ 7 thousands + 4 hundreds + 7 tens

3 Which digit in 28,430 proves that the number is greater than 26,380?

    Ⓐ 2   Ⓑ 8   Ⓒ 4   Ⓓ 3

4 Which number has the greatest digit in the thousands place?

    Ⓐ 47,386   Ⓑ 63,879   Ⓒ 12,782   Ⓓ 51,937

5 Which statements correctly compare two numbers? Select all the correct answers.

    ☐ 649 < 694   ☐ 496 > 469

    ☐ 946 > 964   ☐ 649 > 946

    ☐ 496 < 694   ☐ 469 > 496

6 Place the numbers below in order from lowest to highest. Write 1, 2, 3, and 4 on the lines to show the order.

    ___ 4,087   ___ 4,106   ___ 4,113   ___ 4,068

7 Write the correct number on each blank line.

Which number is ten less than 4,685? _____

Which number is three hundreds more than 25,609? _____

Which number is seven more than 608,542? _____

Which number is three tens more than 1,254? _____

Which number is five hundreds less than 76,659? _____

Which number is one less than 2,555,426? _____

Which number is one hundred less than 554,327? _____

Which number is seven tens less than 877,999? _____

Which number is three thousands less than 265,487? _____

Which number is forty thousand more than 125,335? _____

8 Use the four digits below to create each number described. Each digit should be used exactly once in each number.

$$3 \quad 5 \quad 8 \quad 6$$

The lowest four-digit number possible. _____

The greatest four-digit number possible. _____

A number between 3850 and 3860. _____

A number less than 3,800 that is divisible by 5. _____

The lowest odd number possible. _____

An even number between 5,800 and 5,900. _____

9   Place-value blocks were used to represent a number.

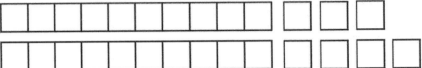

In the space below, draw place-value blocks to represent a number 10 less than the number represented above.

How many blocks of ten would need to be added to represent a number 100 more than the one you drew? _____

How many blocks of ten would need to be added to represent a number 1,000 more than the one you drew? _____

10   Add the symbol <, >, or = to each empty box to make each statement true.

$(8 \times 100) + (6 \times 10) + (3 \times 1)$ ☐ 843

$3 \times 10,000 + 5 \times 1,000 + 6 \times 10 + 2 \times 1$ ☐ 30,562

5 hundreds, 6 tens, and 8 ones ☐ 56 tens and 8 ones

8 ten thousands and 9 tens ☐ 8 thousands and 9 tens

$7,000 + 400 + 80 + 6$ ☐ 7 thousands and 5 hundreds

$6 \times 100,000 + 9 \times 100 + 5 \times 1$ ☐ six hundred thousand and ninety-five

4 thousands and 8 ones ☐ $4 \times 1000 + 8 \times 1$

11   Write numbers on the lines to complete each sentence correctly.

80 is the same as _____ tens.

87 is the same as _____ tens and _____ ones.

Explain how this shows that 87 is greater than 80.

_____

_____

12   Write numbers on the lines to complete each sentence correctly.

297 is the same as _____ hundreds, _____ tens, and _____ ones.

277 is the same as _____ hundreds, _____ tens, and _____ ones.

Explain how this shows that 277 is less than 297.

_____

_____

13   The table shows the population of five different towns.

Greenville	Laketown	Ryde	Warren	Roseland
28,968	26,349	28,715	26,408	28,688

Place the numbers in order from the least to the greatest population.

_____ < _____ < _____ < _____ < _____

The town of Sanford has a population greater than Roseland, but less than Greenville. List four possible populations of Sanford.

_____   _____   _____   _____

Quiz 17: Rounding Whole Numbers

1   If each number is rounded to the nearest thousand, which number will be rounded down?

Ⓐ 4,386   Ⓑ 5,879   Ⓒ 1,782   Ⓓ 8,937

2   What is 784,526 rounded to the nearest ten thousand?

Ⓐ 784,530   Ⓑ 784,500   Ⓒ 780,000   Ⓓ 800,000

3   What is 1,458,700 rounded to the nearest thousand?

Ⓐ 1,400,000   Ⓑ 1,500,000   Ⓒ 1,458,000   Ⓓ 1,459,000

4   Select all the numbers that will equal 860 when rounded to the nearest ten.

☐ 875   ☐ 863   ☐ 868

☐ 853   ☐ 806   ☐ 857

☐ 865   ☐ 881   ☐ 866

5   Select all the numbers that will equal 500 when rounded to the nearest hundred.

☐ 562   ☐ 509   ☐ 524

☐ 435   ☐ 481   ☐ 405

☐ 530   ☐ 557   ☐ 438

6   Round the number 583,726 to each place listed below.

Nearest hundred thousand _____   Nearest ten _____

Nearest ten thousand _____   Nearest hundred _____

7 Complete the table by rounding each number to the nearest 100 and the nearest 1000.

Number	Nearest 100	Nearest 1000
6,387		
5,204		
1,986		
3,259		
64,805		
35,725		
18,133		
25,805		
168,261		
357,909		

8 Complete the table by filling in the missing numbers.

Number Rounded to the Nearest Hundred	Lowest Possible Number	Highest Possible Number
600		
4,200		
68,500		
128,800		
8,745,300		

9 The list below shows an original number and the number after being rounded. Circle the correct place each number has been rounded to.

Number	Rounded Number	Place Rounded		
3,854	3,900	thousand	hundred	ten
24,657	25,000	thousand	hundred	ten
18,534	18,530	thousand	hundred	ten
264,748	265,000	thousand	hundred	ten
756,346	756,300	thousand	hundred	ten

10 The table shows the number of sales a store had on five days.

Day	Monday	Tuesday	Wednesday	Thursday	Friday
Sales	4,087	4,155	4,002	3,995	4,137

For which day will the sales rounded to the nearest thousand be greater than the actual sales? _____

For which day will the sales rounded to the nearest thousand be closest to the actual sales? _____

For which day will the sales rounded to the nearest hundred be 4,200?

_____

For which day will the sales rounded to the nearest ten be 4,140?

_____

For which two days will the sales be the same when rounded to the nearest thousand and hundred? _____ and _____

11 Circle all the numbers below that would be rounded up when rounded to the nearest ten.

36	67	15	82
681	206	365	603
1,674	6,087	5,363	3,426

Explain what all the numbers that are rounded up have in common.

_____

_____

12 Round 185,267 to the nearest ten thousand and the nearest thousand.

Nearest ten thousand _____ Nearest thousand _____

Explain how you worked out whether to round the number up or down.

_____

_____

_____

13 Emiko states that to the nearest thousand, there are 2,000 students at her school. Gary states that there must be at least 2,000 students, but no more than 2,500 students. Describe the mistake that Gary made.

_____

_____

_____

Quiz 18: Adding Whole Numbers

1   What is the sum of 42,387 and 21,592?

    Ⓐ 63,819   Ⓑ 63,879   Ⓒ 63,919   Ⓓ 63,979

2   What is the sum of 685,000 and 215,000?

    Ⓐ 800,000   Ⓑ 890,000   Ⓒ 900,000   Ⓓ 990,000

3   A courier delivered 7,942 small parcels and 9,166 large parcels.

    How many parcels were delivered in all?

    Ⓐ 16,008   Ⓑ 16,108   Ⓒ 17,008   Ⓓ 17,108

4   The table shows how many people saw a play each night.

Night	Number of People
Friday	1,580
Saturday	1,898
Sunday	1,474

    How many people in total went to see the play on the 3 nights?

    Ⓐ 4,742   Ⓑ 4,752   Ⓒ 4,942   Ⓓ 4,952

5   The table shows the male and female population of Vale.

Gender	Population
Male	248,368
Female	267,182

    What is the total population of Vale?

    Ⓐ 405,540   Ⓑ 416,550   Ⓒ 505,440   Ⓓ 515,550

6   An addition statement is shown below.

$$
\begin{array}{r}
3\,5,1\,6\,8 \\
1\,2,1\,7\,4 \\
+\,1\,\square,6\,4\,3 \\
\hline
6\,0,9\,8\,5
\end{array}
$$

What is the missing digit that makes the addition statement true?

Ⓐ 2   Ⓑ 3   Ⓒ 5   Ⓓ 7

7   Which expressions have a sum of 1,000? Select all the correct answers.

☐ 463 + 537   ☐ 756 + 344

☐ 128 + 372 + 289 + 211   ☐ 115 + 285 + 375 + 125

☐ 640 + 235 + 225   ☐ 427 + 398 + 142 + 35

8   Which sum has the greatest value? Select the one correct answer.

☐ 8,962 + 2,467   ☐ 8,564 + 2,735   ☐ 8,943 + 2,593

☐ 8,177 + 2,590   ☐ 8,843 + 2,308   ☐ 8,707 + 2,401

9   Complete the missing number to make each number sentence correct.

62 + _____ = 82   427 + _____ = 477   1,985 + _____ = 7,985

97 + _____ = 137   385 + _____ = 885   6,443 + _____ = 6,743

35 + _____ = 435   917 + _____ = 929   3,011 + _____ = 4,911

48 + _____ = 79   605 + _____ = 4,605   2,464 + _____ = 12,464

89 + _____ = 399   718 + _____ = 6,718   5,557 + _____ = 28,557

10   Complete the addition problems below.

| 459 + | 462 + | 508 + | 235 + |
| 118 | 489 | 374 | 785 |

327 +	615 +	363 +	945 +
489	901	480	983
103	226	117	924

| 6,826 + | 1,485 + | 9,488 + | 6,305 + |
| 1,753 | 2,746 | 4,206 | 9,805 |

2,846 +	4,554 +	5,793 +	7,189 +
1,379	6,221	605	247
467	1,007	531	53

| 36,425 + | 24,508 + | 19,626 + | 77,250 + |
| 24,153 | 28,962 | 17,803 | 36,508 |

| 140,005 + | 648,129 + | 119,763 + | 135,560 + |
| 360,895 | 304,228 | 117,247 | 752,480 |

11   For each addition problem below, complete the calculation in steps. In the first step, add the tens. In the second step, add the ones. In the third step, add the sum of the tens and the ones. The first one has been completed.

Problem	Step 1: Add the Tens	Step 2: Add the Ones	Step 3: Add the Two Sums
63 + 21	60 + 20 = 80	3 + 1 = 4	80 + 4 = 84
29 + 97	____ + ____ = ____	____ + ____ = ____	____ + ____ = ____
41 + 78	____ + ____ = ____	____ + ____ = ____	____ + ____ = ____
86 + 85	____ + ____ = ____	____ + ____ = ____	____ + ____ = ____
75 + 19	____ + ____ = ____	____ + ____ = ____	____ + ____ = ____

12   Find the sum of the three numbers below by adding the hundred thousands, thousands, and hundreds, and then adding the three sums. Write the sum on the line below.

342,000   132,000   214,000

Answer _____

13   In 2012, the state of Colorado had 2,165,983 male residents and 2,135,278 female residents. How many residents were there in all?

Show your work.

Answer _____ residents

Quiz 19: Subtracting Whole Numbers

1   What is the difference of 30,745 and 29,471?

   (A) 274   (B) 374   (C) 1,274   (D) 1,374

2   What is the difference of 214,000 and 86,000?

   (A) 128,000   (B) 138,000   (C) 172,000   (D) 178,000

3   The normal price of a car is $15,900. During a sale, the car is $1,499 less than the normal price. What is the sale price?

   (A) $14,401   (B) $14,501   (C) $14,509   (D) $15,599

4   A subtraction statement is shown below.

$$
\begin{array}{r}
3\,5,9\,6\,2 \\
-\ 2\,\square,1\,0\,4 \\
\hline
8,8\,5\,8
\end{array}
$$

What is the missing digit that makes the statement true?

   (A) 3   (B) 5   (C) 7   (D) 9

5   Belinda's florist business pays a rent that goes up by a set amount each year. The table shows the rent for three different years.

Year	Rent
2012	$18,980
2013	$19,760
2014	$20,540

By how much does the rent go up each year?

   (A) $780   (B) $880   (C) $1,780   (D) $1,880

6 Which expressions have a difference of 40? Select all the correct answers.

☐ 2,980 – 940 ☐ 3,570 – 3,530 ☐ 299 – 200 – 59

☐ 13,480 – 13,080 ☐ 687 – 640 – 7 ☐ 1,000 – 600 – 60

7 Which difference is equal to 400? Select the one correct answer.

☐ 79,875 – 75,875 ☐ 79,875 – 79,835 ☐ 79,875 – 79,475

☐ 79,875 – 39,875 ☐ 79,875 – 79,871 ☐ 79,875 – 75,475

8 Complete the missing number to make each number sentence correct.

98 – _____ = 38 869 – _____ = 469 4,672 – _____ = 2,672

66 – _____ = 36 738 – _____ = 718 8,391 – _____ = 8,311

57 – _____ = 52 556 – _____ = 550 1,487 – _____ = 1,087

528 – _____ = 28 467 – _____ = 62 9,770 – _____ = 770

341 – _____ = 301 941 – _____ = 521 5,169 – _____ = 3,069

9 Which number is 4,000 less than 4,896,320? _____

Which number is 300 less than 4,896,320? _____

Which number is 50,000 less than 4,896,320? _____

Which number is 600,000 less than 4,896,320? _____

Which number is 2,000,000 less than 4,896,320? _____

Which number is 20 less than 4,896,320? _____

10   Complete the subtraction problems below.

685 −	378 −	598 −	401 −
193	281	399	257

655 −	776 −	547 −	980 −
121	325	295	526
423	218	104	173

7,608 −	8,009 −	6,167 −	4,276 −
1,256	1,474	823	856
397	3,155	195	72

299,555 −	762,843 −	228,495 −	675,891 −
142,005	254,217	228,188	65,345

11   The table shows the total sales of a juice bar for each season.

Season	Spring	Summer	Fall	Winter
Sales ($)	27,874	25,655	16,904	14,337

How much more is made in spring and summer than in winter and fall?

Show your work.

Answer $_____

12   The table shows the population of Ohio for different age groups.

Age (years)	Number of People
Under 5	754,930
5 to 24	3,189,953
25 to 44	3,325,210
45 to 64	2,575,290
65 to 84	1,330,961
85 and over	176,796

What is the difference between the number of people aged 25 to 44 and the number of people aged 45 to 64?

Show your work.

Answer _____ people

What is the difference between the number of people aged 65 to 84 and the number of people aged 85 and over?

Show your work.

Answer _____ people

How many more people are there aged under 5 than aged 85 and over?

Show your work.

Answer _____ people

Quiz 20: Multiplying Whole Numbers

1   What is the value of 48 times 9?

ⓐ 368   ⓑ 432   ⓒ 471   ⓓ 992

2   What is the product of 1,425 and 4?

ⓐ 4,600   ⓑ 4,700   ⓒ 5,600   ⓓ 5,700

3   The 18 members of a science club put in $12 each so the club could buy a solar kit. How much was the solar kit?

ⓐ $116   ⓑ $196   ⓒ $216   ⓓ $228

4   Which expressions have a value of 480? Select all the correct answers.

☐ (6 × 8) × 10   ☐ 160 × 30   ☐ (40 × 10) + (80 × 10)

☐ 24 × 20   ☐ 120 × 6   ☐ 40 × 80

5   Lionel jogs for 45 minutes every afternoon. Complete the table to show how long he jogs for in total for each number of days.

Number of Days	Total Number of Minutes
5	
7	
14	
30	
45	
60	

6 Complete each number sentence by writing the missing number on the blank line.

$7 \times 9 = $ _____ $8 \times 4 = $ _____ $6 \times 6 = $ _____

$21 \times 4 = $ _____ $20 \times 6 = $ _____ $11 \times 9 = $ _____

$33 \times 2 = $ _____ $40 \times 9 = $ _____ $22 \times 3 = $ _____

$60 \times 50 = $ _____ $20 \times 70 = $ _____ $80 \times 40 = $ _____

7 Complete the multiplication problems below.

$$
\begin{array}{r} 37 \\ \times\ 5 \\ \hline \end{array}
\qquad
\begin{array}{r} 68 \\ \times\ 6 \\ \hline \end{array}
\qquad
\begin{array}{r} 29 \\ \times\ 4 \\ \hline \end{array}
\qquad
\begin{array}{r} 45 \\ \times\ 8 \\ \hline \end{array}
$$

$$
\begin{array}{r} 265 \\ \times\ 3 \\ \hline \end{array}
\qquad
\begin{array}{r} 192 \\ \times\ 4 \\ \hline \end{array}
\qquad
\begin{array}{r} 504 \\ \times\ 9 \\ \hline \end{array}
\qquad
\begin{array}{r} 255 \\ \times\ 7 \\ \hline \end{array}
$$

$$
\begin{array}{r} 5{,}091 \\ \times\ 5 \\ \hline \end{array}
\qquad
\begin{array}{r} 7{,}634 \\ \times\ 8 \\ \hline \end{array}
\qquad
\begin{array}{r} 2{,}009 \\ \times\ 3 \\ \hline \end{array}
\qquad
\begin{array}{r} 8{,}651 \\ \times\ 6 \\ \hline \end{array}
$$

$$
\begin{array}{r} 71 \\ \times\ 45 \\ \hline \end{array}
\qquad
\begin{array}{r} 13 \\ \times\ 26 \\ \hline \end{array}
\qquad
\begin{array}{r} 48 \\ \times\ 34 \\ \hline \end{array}
\qquad
\begin{array}{r} 92 \\ \times\ 78 \\ \hline \end{array}
$$

Quiz 21: Understanding and Representing Multiplication

1 Which of these does the model below represent?

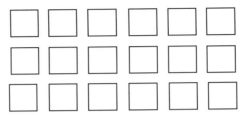

Ⓐ 3 × 2 = 6   Ⓑ 6 × 2 = 12   Ⓒ 3 × 6 = 18   Ⓓ 18 × 2 = 36

2 Which expression has the same value as 95 × 6?

Ⓐ (9 × 6) + (5 × 6)   Ⓑ 95 × 3 × 3

Ⓒ 90 + (5 × 6)   Ⓓ 95 + 95 + 95 + 95 + 95 + 95

3 Which expression has the greatest value?

Ⓐ 149 × 6   Ⓑ 149 × 4   Ⓒ 149 × 7   Ⓓ 149 × 3

4 The table shows the relationship between feet and inches. Complete the table by showing how many inches are in 9, 14, and 27 feet.

Feet	3	7	9	14	27
Inches	36	84			

5 Complete the number sentence to show the calculation modeled by the base-ten blocks below.

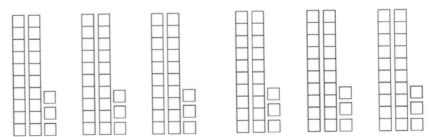

Answer _____ × _____ = _____

6   Which pairs of numbers could be added to this table? Select all the possible answers.

Number	Number × 100
850	85,000
3,501	350,100
19	1,900

☐ 28 and 2008   ☐ 365 and 36,500

☐ 1,987 and 19,870   ☐ 60,004 and 6,000,400

☐ 495 and 4,0095   ☐ 8,703 and 8,703,000

7   Complete the area model to find the value of each expression below.

27 x 43

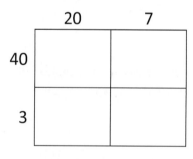

Answer _____

64 × 82

80   60   4
2

Answer _____

95 x 35

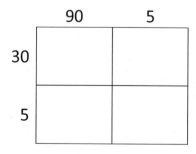

Answer _____

59 × 76

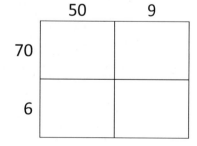

Answer _____

8   Complete the number sentences by writing the missing number in each blank space. Then complete the calculation.

$68 \times 9 = (60 \times 9) + (\underline{\quad} \times 9)$

= \underline{\qquad} + \underline{\qquad}

= \underline{\qquad}

$37 \times 6 = (30 \times 6) + (\underline{\quad} \times 6)$

= \underline{\qquad} + \underline{\qquad}

= \underline{\qquad}

$72 \times 8 = (\underline{\quad} \times 8) + (\underline{\quad} \times 8)$

= \underline{\qquad} + \underline{\qquad}

= \underline{\qquad}

$94 \times 5 = (\underline{\quad} \times 5) + (\underline{\quad} \times 5)$

= \underline{\qquad} + \underline{\qquad}

= \underline{\qquad}

$53 \times 7 = (\underline{\quad} \times \underline{\quad}) + (\underline{\quad} \times \underline{\quad})$

= \underline{\qquad} + \underline{\qquad}

= \underline{\qquad}

$85 \times 4 = (\underline{\quad} \times \underline{\quad}) + (\underline{\quad} \times \underline{\quad})$

= \underline{\qquad} + \underline{\qquad}

= \underline{\qquad}

9   Sawyer ordered 14 shirts for his basketball team. Each shirt cost $29. Complete the equation to show how to find the total cost of the shirts. Then write the answer below.

\underline{\qquad} $\times$ \underline{\qquad} = \underline{\qquad}

Answer $\$\underline{\qquad\qquad}$

10   An artist sold 7 paintings one month. Each painting sold for $659. What was the total amount made from the sale of the paintings? Write and solve an equation to show how to find the answer.

Answer $\$\underline{\qquad\qquad}$

11 Xavier tiles the top of a table with 3 rows of 4 tiles each.

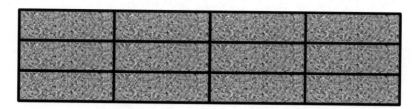

Each tile has an area of 48 square inches. What is the total area of the top of the table? Use words or equations to show how you found your answer.

Answer _____ square inches

12 On the grid below, shade a rectangle that can be used to find the product of 16 and 7.

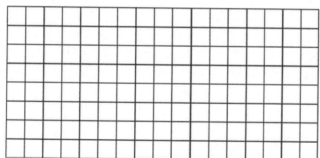

What is the product of 16 and 7? _____

Explain how the shaded rectangle can be used to find the product.

_____

_____

_____

Quiz 22: Dividing Whole Numbers

1 What is 969 divided by 3?

Ⓐ 323 Ⓑ 326 Ⓒ 328 Ⓓ 329

2 What is 287 divided by 7?

Ⓐ 39 Ⓑ 41 Ⓒ 43 Ⓓ 47

3 Which number makes the equation below true?

$$4,824 \div \underline{\quad} = 804$$

Ⓐ 6 Ⓑ 7 Ⓒ 8 Ⓓ 9

4 Wendy gets paid $9 for each hour she works. She earned $414 for one week's work. How many hours did Wendy work that week?

Ⓐ 42 Ⓑ 44 Ⓒ 46 Ⓓ 48

5 A farm has 8,400 square meters of fields divided into 6 equal sections. What is the area of each section?

Answer _____ square meters

6 Which expressions have a value of 26? Select all the correct answers.

☐ 108 ÷ 3 ☐ 104 ÷ 4 ☐ 224 ÷ 8

☐ 168 ÷ 6 ☐ 216 ÷ 9 ☐ 182 ÷ 7

7 Which numbers can be evenly divided by 4? Select all the correct answers.

☐ 625 ☐ 408 ☐ 332

☐ 801 ☐ 577 ☐ 190

8 Complete each number sentence by writing the missing number on the blank line.

$64 \div 2 =$ _____ $99 \div 3 =$ _____ $84 \div 4 =$ _____

$882 \div 2 =$ _____ $396 \div 3 =$ _____ $660 \div 6 =$ _____

$4{,}248 \div 2 =$ _____ $8{,}488 \div 4 =$ _____ $7{,}007 \div 7 =$ _____

$2{,}500 \div 5 =$ _____ $9{,}900 \div 9 =$ _____ $3{,}906 \div 3 =$ _____

9 Complete the division problems below.

$9 \overline{)639}$ $3 \overline{)885}$ $4 \overline{)768}$

$5 \overline{)775}$ $6 \overline{)516}$ $7 \overline{)581}$

$4 \overline{)5416}$ $7 \overline{)4571}$ $9 \overline{)6354}$

Quiz 23: Understanding and Representing Division

1   What is the value of 4900 ÷ 7?

Ⓐ 70   Ⓑ 90   Ⓒ 700   Ⓓ 900

2   Which of these shows a correct way to find 360 ÷ 4 ÷ 6?

Ⓐ 360 ÷ (6 - 4) = 180   Ⓑ 360 ÷ 6 = 60, 60 × 4 = 240

Ⓒ 360 ÷ 6 = 60, 60 ÷ 4 = 15   Ⓓ 6 + 4 = 10, 360 ÷ 10 = 36

3   Which of these could be used to find the value of p in 4 × p = 948?

Ⓐ 948 ÷ 4 = p Ⓑ 4 ÷ 948 = p Ⓒ 948 × 4 = p Ⓓ p ÷ 948 = 4

4   Which of these describes a situation where there will be 5 students left over?

Ⓐ 74 students divided into 7 equal groups

Ⓑ 83 students divided into 9 equal groups

Ⓒ 59 students divided into 6 equal groups

Ⓓ 67 students divided into 8 equal groups

5   The diagram below shows how 32 desks are organized.

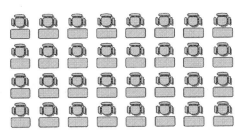

Which of these does the diagram show? Select all the correct answers.

☐ 32 × 4 = 128   ☐ 32 ÷ 8 = 4   ☐ 8 × 4 = 32

☐ 32 ÷ 4 = 8   ☐ 4 × 8 = 32   ☐ 128 ÷ 4 = 32

6 For each division equation, write a multiplication equation that could be used to check the answer.

$392 \div 4 = 98$ _____ × _____ = _____

$865 \div 5 = 173$ _____ × _____ = _____

$522 \div 6 = 87$ _____ × _____ = _____

$928 \div 8 = 116$ _____ × _____ = _____

$1{,}778 \div 7 = 254$ _____ × _____ = _____

$3{,}870 \div 9 = 430$ _____ × _____ = _____

7 Students shaded the number of squares on a grid listed below.

Hayley, 153   Wade, 112   Sanjay, 184   Eva, 155

Who could have shaded a rectangle that was 5 squares long? How many squares high would the shape be? Show or explain your answer.

Student _____   **Height** _____ squares

Who could have shaded a rectangle that was 9 squares long? How many squares high would the shape be? Show or explain your answer.

Student _____   **Height** _____ squares

Which two students could have shaded a rectangles 8 squares long? What would be the difference in height between the two rectangles? Show or explain your answer.

Students _____ and _____

Difference in height _____ squares

8   The diagram represents how Baker has sorted 38 cans of soup into groups.

Complete the division equation that describes how the cans are sorted.

38 ÷ ___ = ___ r ___

Explain what the equation tells about how the cans are sorted.

_____

_____

9   Ronald has 60 quarters. He spends 8 quarters each day on his lunch. Use the coins below to complete a model that shows how many days he can spend 8 quarters for. Circle groups of coins to complete the model.

How many days can he spend 8 quarters for? _____ days

How many quarters will be left over? _____ quarters

10   Joel estimates that 139 divided by 4 will be about 35, and that 897 divided by 3 will be about 300. Show the calculations that Joel completed to make the estimations.

_____ ÷ _____ = 35   _____ ÷ _____ = 300

11 The table shows the number of tickets sold to an ice hockey game.

Type of Ticket	Adult Tickets	Children's Tickets
Basic	3,852	2,408
Special		

There were 6 times fewer special adult tickets sold than basic adult tickets. How many special adult tickets were sold?

Show your work.

Answer _____ tickets

There were 7 times fewer special children's tickets sold than basic children's tickets. How many special children's tickets were sold?

Show your work.

Answer _____ tickets

Of all the adults at the game, 1 out of 6 were supporting the away team. How many adults were supporting the away team?

Show your work.

Answer _____ adults

Quizzes 24 to 36

Number and Operations – Fractions

Directions

Read each question carefully. For each multiple-choice question, fill in the circle for the correct answer. For other types of questions, follow the directions given in the question.

You may use a ruler to help you answer questions. You should answer the questions without using a calculator.

MATHEMATICS SKILLS LIST
For Parents, Teachers, and Tutors

Quizzes 24 through 36 cover these skills from the Georgia Standards of Excellence.

Number and Operations – Fractions

Extend understanding of fraction equivalence and ordering.

1. Explain why two or more fractions are equivalent by using visual fraction models. Focus attention on how the number and size of the parts differ even though the fractions themselves are the same size. Use this principle to recognize and generate equivalent fractions.
2. Compare two fractions with different numerators and different denominators, e.g., by using visual fraction models, by creating common denominators or numerators, or by comparing to a benchmark fraction such as 1/2. Recognize that comparisons are valid only when the two fractions refer to the same whole. Record the results of comparisons with symbols >, =, or <, and justify the conclusions.

Build fractions from unit fractions.

3. Understand a fraction a/b with a numerator > 1 as a sum of unit fractions $1/b$.
   a. Understand addition and subtraction of fractions as joining and separating parts referring to the same whole.
   b. Decompose a fraction into a sum of fractions with the same denominator in more than one way, recording each decomposition by an equation. Justify decompositions.
   c. Add and subtract mixed numbers with like denominators, e.g., by replacing each mixed number with an equivalent fraction, and/or by using properties of operations and the relationship between addition and subtraction.
   d. Solve word problems involving addition and subtraction of fractions referring to the same whole and having like denominators.
4. Apply and extend previous understandings of multiplication to multiply a fraction by a whole number.
   a. Understand a fraction a/b as a multiple of $1/b$.
   b. Understand a multiple of a/b as a multiple of $1/b$, and use this understanding to multiply a fraction by a whole number.
   c. Solve word problems involving multiplication of a fraction by a whole number.

Understand decimal notation for fractions, and compare decimal fractions.

5. Express a fraction with denominator 10 as an equivalent fraction with denominator 100, and use this technique to add two fractions with respective denominators 10 and 100.
6. Use decimal notation for fractions with denominators 10 or 100.
7. Compare two decimals to hundredths by reasoning about their size. Recognize that comparisons are valid only when the two decimals refer to the same whole. Record the results of comparisons with the symbols >, =, or <, and justify the conclusions, e.g., by using a visual model.

Quiz 24: Understanding Equivalent Fractions

1   What fraction of the figure below is shaded?

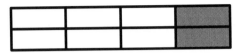

     Ⓐ $\frac{1}{2}$ Ⓑ $\frac{1}{3}$ Ⓒ $\frac{1}{4}$ Ⓓ $\frac{3}{4}$

2   Which fraction is equivalent to the shaded area of the rectangle?

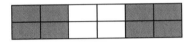

     Ⓐ $\frac{1}{2}$ Ⓑ $\frac{3}{4}$ Ⓒ $\frac{2}{3}$ Ⓓ $\frac{1}{3}$

3   Which fraction could the point on the number line represent? Select all the possible answers.

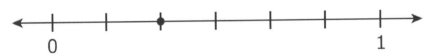

  ☐ $\frac{6}{10}$ ☐ $\frac{2}{6}$ ☐ $\frac{1}{3}$ ☐ $\frac{2}{4}$

  ☐ $\frac{3}{8}$ ☐ $\frac{4}{12}$ ☐ $\frac{1}{6}$ ☐ $\frac{4}{10}$

4   Mr. Hamlin owns 4 spotted bow ties and 16 plain bow ties.

Complete the fractions that show the fraction of bow ties that are plain.

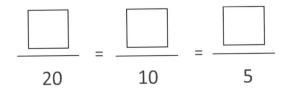

$$\frac{\square}{20} = \frac{\square}{10} = \frac{\square}{5}$$

5 Shade half of each model below. Then use the model to complete the fractions equivalent to $\frac{1}{2}$.

    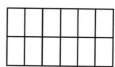

$\frac{1}{2}$ $\frac{}{4}$ $\frac{}{6}$ $\frac{}{8}$ $\frac{}{12}$

6 Shade the diagrams below to show the fraction $\frac{2}{5}$ and a fraction equivalent to $\frac{2}{5}$. Then write the equivalent fraction for the second diagram.

Fraction $\frac{2}{5}$ 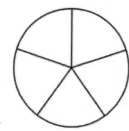   Fraction $\frac{}{}$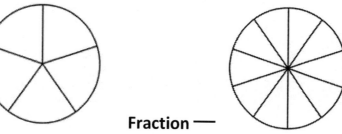

7 Shade the model below to show the fraction $\frac{4}{12}$.

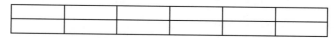

Shade the model below to show a fraction equivalent to $\frac{4}{12}$.

What fraction is shaded above? _____

Shade the model below to show a fraction equivalent to $\frac{4}{12}$.

What fraction is shaded above? _____

8   Violet has 20 candies. She divides them into 5 equal groups.

What fraction of the total candies is each group? _____

Emilio has 10 candies. He divides them into 5 equal groups.

What fraction of the total candies is each group? _____

Complete the two equivalent fractions represented by Violet's and Emilio's candies.

$$\frac{\boxed{}}{20} = \frac{\boxed{}}{10}$$

9   Plot the fraction $\frac{2}{3}$ on the first number line. Then plot two fractions equivalent to $\frac{2}{3}$ on the second and third number lines.

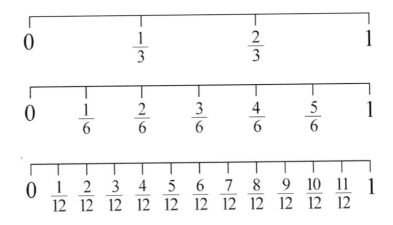

What two equivalent fractions did you plot? _____ and _____

10   Plot the fraction $\frac{4}{5}$ on the number line below. Then plot a fraction equivalent to $\frac{4}{5}$ on the second number line.

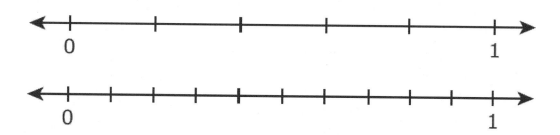

What fraction did you plot on the second number line? _____

Explain how the number lines show that the two fractions are equivalent.

_____

_____

_____

11   Divide the rectangles below into parts to show that $\frac{5}{6}$ is equivalent to $\frac{10}{12}$.

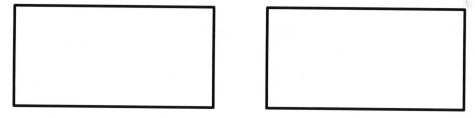

Explain how the diagrams show that the two fractions are equivalent.

_____

_____

_____

Quiz 25: Identifying and Generating Equivalent Fractions

1   Which fraction is equivalent to $\frac{8}{12}$?

   Ⓐ $\frac{2}{3}$ Ⓑ $\frac{2}{6}$ Ⓒ $\frac{1}{4}$ Ⓓ $\frac{1}{3}$

2   Which fraction is equivalent to the shaded area of the rectangle?

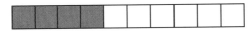

   Ⓐ $\frac{4}{6}$ Ⓑ $\frac{2}{10}$ Ⓒ $\frac{2}{3}$ Ⓓ $\frac{2}{5}$

3   Which model is shaded to show a fraction equivalent to $\frac{1}{3}$?

Ⓐ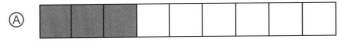

Ⓑ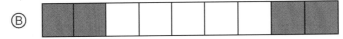

Ⓒ

Ⓓ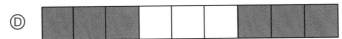

4   Which fraction can be simplified to a simpler form?

   Ⓐ $\frac{3}{100}$ Ⓑ $\frac{21}{100}$ Ⓒ $\frac{25}{100}$ Ⓓ $\frac{31}{100}$

5   Which figure is shaded to represent a fraction equivalent to the model below?

Ⓐ 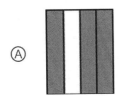   Ⓑ 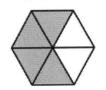   Ⓒ    Ⓓ

6 Which pairs of fractions below are equivalent? Select all the correct answers.

☐ $\frac{2}{6}$ and $\frac{2}{12}$ ☐ $\frac{3}{6}$ and $\frac{6}{8}$ ☐ $\frac{1}{3}$ and $\frac{2}{6}$ ☐ $\frac{4}{5}$ and $\frac{8}{10}$

☐ $\frac{1}{4}$ and $\frac{2}{5}$ ☐ $\frac{3}{4}$ and $\frac{9}{12}$ ☐ $\frac{1}{5}$ and $\frac{1}{10}$ ☐ $\frac{2}{4}$ and $\frac{50}{100}$

7 Complete the calculations to find three fractions equivalent to $\frac{3}{4}$.

$$\frac{3}{4} \times \frac{2}{2} = ---$$ $$\frac{3}{4} \times \frac{3}{3} = ---$$ $$\frac{3}{4} \times \frac{5}{5} = ---$$

8 For each hundreds grid below, shade the diagram below it so that the same fraction of the shape is shaded. Then write the two fractions you shaded.

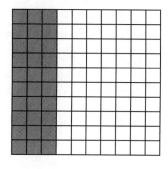 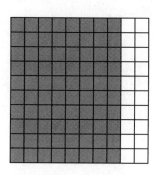 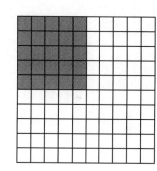

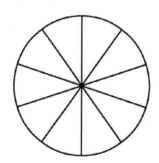 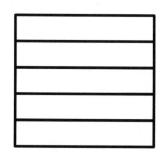 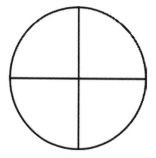

$$\overline{}{100}, \overline{}{10}$$ $$\overline{}{100}, \overline{}{5}$$ $$\overline{}{100}, \overline{}{4}$$

9 Use the number lines below to show that $\frac{1}{3}$, $\frac{2}{6}$, and $\frac{4}{12}$ are equivalent.

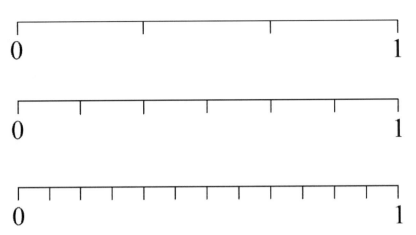

Explain how the number lines show that the fractions are equivalent.

_____

_____

_____

10 Circle all the fractions that can be simplified to an equivalent fraction.

$$\frac{5}{7} \qquad \frac{6}{12} \qquad \frac{3}{10} \qquad \frac{1}{5} \qquad \frac{4}{6} \qquad \frac{75}{100} \qquad \frac{7}{8}$$

For each fraction you circled, write the fraction in lowest form below.

Explain why the fractions you did not circle cannot be simplified.

_____

_____

_____

11 Alvin, Ben, and Drake were practicing soccer. They each took some shots at goal. Their results are described below.

- Alvin took 6 shots and scored 4 goals.
- Ben took 12 shots and scored the same fraction of goals as Alvin.
- Drake took 3 shots and scored the same fraction of goals as Alvin.

Complete the table below to show the goals scored and missed by Ben and Drake.

Soccer Goals

Alvin	Ben	Drake
✓ ✓ ✓ ✓ ✗ ✗		

✓ = goal scored   ✗ = goal missed

Complete the fractions to show the goals scored and missed by Ben and Drake.

Ben $\dfrac{}{12}$ scored, $\dfrac{}{12}$ missed   **Drake** $\dfrac{}{3}$ scored, $\dfrac{}{3}$ missed

12 Janelle answered 80 out of 100 questions on a quiz correctly. She answered the same fraction of questions correctly on a bonus quiz with 5 questions. How many questions on the bonus quiz did she answer correctly? Show or explain how you found your answer.

Answer _____ questions

Quiz 26: Comparing Fractions

1 Which fraction below is the greatest?

Ⓐ $\frac{7}{12}$ Ⓑ $\frac{1}{4}$ Ⓒ $\frac{2}{3}$ Ⓓ $\frac{5}{6}$

2 What do the shaded models below show?

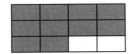 

Ⓐ $\frac{10}{12} > \frac{2}{3}$ Ⓑ $\frac{1}{3} > \frac{5}{6}$ Ⓒ $\frac{1}{12} > \frac{1}{3}$ Ⓓ $\frac{5}{6} = \frac{2}{3}$

3 Which number sentence is true?

Ⓐ $\frac{5}{8} > \frac{3}{4}$ Ⓑ $\frac{1}{6} > \frac{1}{3}$ Ⓒ $\frac{10}{12} < \frac{3}{4}$ Ⓓ $\frac{5}{12} < \frac{1}{2}$

4 Place the fractions below in order from smallest to greatest. Write the numbers 1, 2, 3, and 4 on the lines to show the order.

_____ $\frac{3}{5}$ _____ $\frac{3}{10}$ _____ $\frac{7}{10}$ _____ $\frac{4}{5}$

5 Which fractions can be placed in the empty box to make the statement below true? Select all the correct answers.

$$\frac{1}{4} < \boxed{}$$

☐ $\frac{5}{6}$ ☐ $\frac{3}{4}$ ☐ $\frac{1}{3}$ ☐ $\frac{1}{6}$

☐ $\frac{1}{2}$ ☐ $\frac{1}{8}$ ☐ $\frac{1}{10}$ ☐ $\frac{3}{12}$

6 Rewrite the fractions below as fractions with the denominator 12.

$$\frac{2}{3} =$$

$$\frac{3}{4} =$$

$$\frac{1}{2} =$$

$$\frac{5}{6} =$$

Use the fractions you wrote to place the fractions below in order from lowest to highest. Write the fractions on the lines.

$$\frac{2}{3}, \frac{3}{4}, \frac{1}{2}, \frac{5}{6}, \frac{7}{12}, \frac{5}{12}$$

Lowest   **Highest**

———   ———   ———   ———   ———   ———

7 Place the list of fractions below in order from lowest to highest. Show your work or explain how you found your answer.

$$\frac{4}{5}, \frac{7}{10}, \frac{9}{10}, \frac{21}{25}, \frac{85}{100}, \frac{3}{5}$$

Lowest   **Highest**

———   ———   ———   ———   ———   ———

8 Write the symbol <, >, or = in the empty box to make each statement correct. Then shade the diagram to show that the statement is correct.

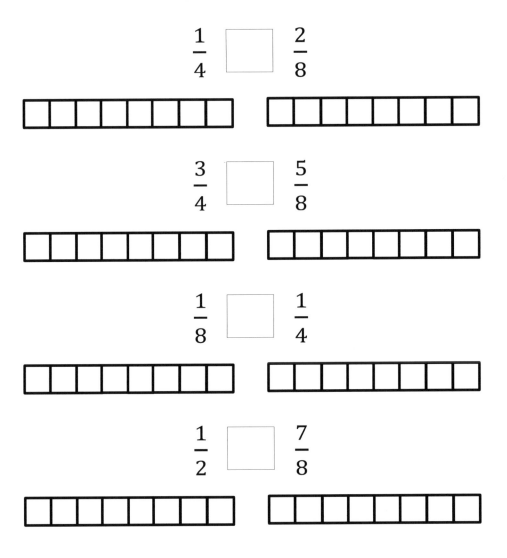

$$\frac{1}{4} \quad \square \quad \frac{2}{8}$$

$$\frac{3}{4} \quad \square \quad \frac{5}{8}$$

$$\frac{1}{8} \quad \square \quad \frac{1}{4}$$

$$\frac{1}{2} \quad \square \quad \frac{7}{8}$$

9 Mark lives $\frac{3}{4}$ miles from school. Campbell lives $\frac{5}{6}$ miles from school. Audrey lives $\frac{7}{12}$ miles from school. Who lives closest to the school?

Show your work.

Answer _____

10 Circle all the fractions below that are greater than $\frac{1}{2}$.

$$\frac{9}{10} \qquad \frac{3}{4} \qquad \frac{2}{12} \qquad \frac{1}{6} \qquad \frac{3}{8} \qquad \frac{5}{10} \qquad \frac{7}{12} \qquad \frac{20}{100}$$

Explain how you can compare the numerator and denominator to determine if each fraction is greater than $\frac{1}{2}$.

_____

_____

Which fraction listed is equal to $\frac{1}{2}$? _____

Explain how you can compare the numerator and denominator to determine which fraction is equal to $\frac{1}{2}$.

_____

_____

11 Divide the rectangle below into 6 equal areas. Shade $\frac{5}{6}$ of the rectangle.

Divide the rectangle below into 12 equal areas. Shade $\frac{7}{12}$ of the rectangle.

Use the shaded models to compare the fractions $\frac{5}{6}$ and $\frac{7}{12}$.

_____

_____

Quiz 27: Understanding Addition and Subtraction of Fractions

1   What is the value of $\frac{3}{10} + \frac{6}{10}$?

   Ⓐ $\frac{9}{10}$ Ⓑ $\frac{9}{20}$ Ⓒ $\frac{9}{100}$ Ⓓ $\frac{18}{100}$

2   What is the value of $\frac{9}{12} - \frac{3}{12}$?

   Ⓐ $\frac{1}{12}$ Ⓑ $\frac{3}{12}$ Ⓒ $\frac{5}{12}$ Ⓓ $\frac{6}{12}$

3   Which of these is the same as the shaded fraction below?

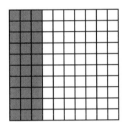

   Ⓐ $\frac{1}{3} + \frac{1}{3} + \frac{1}{3}$ Ⓑ $\frac{1}{10} + \frac{1}{10} + \frac{1}{10}$

   Ⓒ $\frac{1}{30} + \frac{1}{30} + \frac{1}{30}$ Ⓓ $\frac{3}{100} + \frac{3}{100} + \frac{3}{100}$

4   Which shaded model shows a fraction $\frac{1}{10}$ less than $\frac{2}{5}$?

Ⓐ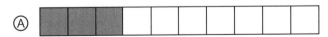

Ⓑ

Ⓒ

Ⓓ

5   What is the difference of $\frac{7}{10}$ and $\frac{4}{10}$?

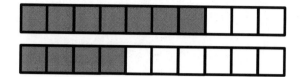

Answer _____

6   Convert the fractions for each sum or difference to fractions with the same denominator. Then complete the calculation.

$\frac{2}{3} + \frac{1}{6}$ $\dfrac{}{6} + \dfrac{}{6} = \dfrac{}{}$

$\frac{1}{2} + \frac{3}{12}$ $\dfrac{}{12} + \dfrac{}{12} = \dfrac{}{}$

$\frac{4}{5} + \frac{1}{10}$ $\dfrac{}{} + \dfrac{}{} = \dfrac{}{}$

$\frac{11}{12} - \frac{3}{4}$ $\dfrac{}{} - \dfrac{}{} = \dfrac{}{}$

$\frac{7}{8} - \frac{1}{2}$ $\dfrac{}{} - \dfrac{}{} = \dfrac{}{}$

$\frac{1}{3} + \frac{2}{6} + \frac{3}{12}$ $\dfrac{}{12} + \dfrac{}{12} + \dfrac{}{12} = \dfrac{}{}$

$\frac{3}{5} + \frac{3}{10} + \frac{7}{100}$ $\dfrac{}{} + \dfrac{}{} + \dfrac{}{} = \dfrac{}{}$

$\frac{3}{4} - \frac{1}{6} - \frac{5}{12}$ $\dfrac{}{} - \dfrac{}{} - \dfrac{}{} = \dfrac{}{}$

7   Shade the models below to find the sum given. Then write the answer on the blank line.

Sum	**Model**	**Answer**
$\dfrac{1}{3} + \dfrac{1}{3}$		_____
$\dfrac{1}{5} + \dfrac{2}{5}$	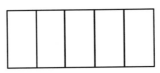	_____
$\dfrac{1}{6} + \dfrac{3}{6}$	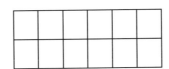	_____
$\dfrac{3}{12} + \dfrac{1}{12} + \dfrac{2}{12}$		_____

8   Shade the models below to find the difference given. Then write the answer on the blank line.

Difference	**Model**	**Answer**
$\dfrac{3}{4} - \dfrac{1}{4}$		_____
$\dfrac{7}{8} - \dfrac{5}{8}$	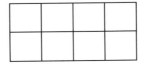	_____
$\dfrac{10}{12} - \dfrac{3}{12} - \dfrac{4}{12}$	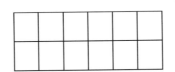	_____

9   At the start of the week, a plant had a height of $\frac{5}{8}$ inches. The plant grew $\frac{1}{4}$ of an inch during the week. Shade the diagram below to represent the height of the plant at the end of the week.

What was the height of the plant at the end of the week? _____ inches

10   Jamie read for $\frac{1}{2}$ an hour before school, $\frac{1}{4}$ of an hour on his lunch break, and $\frac{3}{4}$ of an hour after school. Use the number line below to find how long he read for in all. Write your answer on the line below.

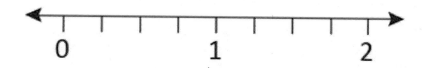

Answer _____ hours

11   Kendra has two cartons of juice. The orange carton has $\frac{5}{8}$ ounces of juice. The pineapple carton has $\frac{3}{4}$ ounces of juice. She mixes the two juices together. Then she drinks $\frac{1}{2}$ an ounce of juice. How much of the juice mix remains?

Show your work.

Answer _____ ounces

Quiz 28: Decomposing Fractions

1   Which expression represents the fraction of the figure that is shaded?

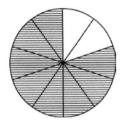

Ⓐ $\frac{1}{10} + \frac{1}{10} + \frac{1}{10}$ Ⓑ $\frac{3}{10} + \frac{3}{10} + \frac{3}{10}$

Ⓒ $\frac{6}{10} + \frac{2}{10} + \frac{2}{10}$ Ⓓ $\frac{3}{10} + \frac{2}{10} + \frac{3}{10}$

2   Wesley has completed $\frac{5}{8}$ of his science project. What fraction of the science project remains?

Ⓐ $\frac{8}{5}$ Ⓑ $\frac{1}{8}$ Ⓒ $\frac{3}{8}$ Ⓓ $\frac{3}{5}$

3   Eleanor cuts a piece of cardboard into 10 equal strips. She uses 4 pieces to make name tags. She divides the remaining pieces into 2 equal groups, and makes a bookmark with the pieces in each equal group.

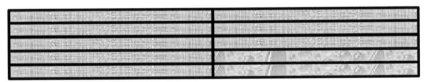

What fraction of the total cardboard is used to make each bookmark?

Ⓐ $\frac{2}{10}$ Ⓑ $\frac{3}{10}$ Ⓒ $\frac{5}{10}$ Ⓓ $\frac{6}{10}$

4   Which expressions have a sum equal to $\frac{5}{6}$? Select all the correct answers.

☐ $\frac{1}{6} + \frac{5}{6}$ ☐ $\frac{2}{3} + \frac{3}{3}$ ☐ $\frac{2}{6} + \frac{3}{6}$

☐ $\frac{1}{2} + \frac{5}{3}$ ☐ $\frac{1}{6} + \frac{4}{6}$ ☐ $\frac{5}{3} + \frac{5}{3}$

5   Complete the missing fraction in each sum.

$$\frac{3}{6} + \quad = \frac{5}{6} \qquad \frac{4}{8} + \quad = \frac{5}{8} \qquad \frac{1}{3} + \quad = \frac{3}{3}$$

$$\frac{5}{12} + \quad = \frac{11}{12} \qquad \frac{2}{10} + \quad = \frac{9}{10} \qquad \frac{2}{5} + \quad = \frac{4}{5}$$

6   Complete the missing fraction in each difference.

$$\frac{5}{6} - \quad = \frac{2}{6} \qquad \frac{7}{10} - \quad = \frac{3}{10} \qquad \frac{8}{12} - \quad = \frac{2}{12}$$

$$\frac{4}{5} - \quad = \frac{3}{5} \qquad \frac{6}{8} - \quad = \frac{2}{8} \qquad \frac{12}{100} - \quad = \frac{1}{100}$$

7   Shade the diagrams below to show how many eighths are in one quarter. Complete the equation to show how many eighths are in one quarter.

Equation $+$ $= \frac{1}{4}$

Shade the diagrams below to show how many tenths are in two fifths. Then write an equation to show how many tenths are in two fifths.

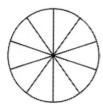 

Equation

8 Shade the first fraction model below to show the fraction that makes the sum equal to 1. Then complete the missing fraction in the equation.

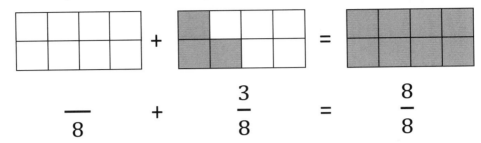

$$\frac{}{8} \quad + \quad \frac{3}{8} \quad = \quad \frac{8}{8}$$

9 Shade the diagrams below to show two equal fractions that add to 1. Then write an equation to show the sum of the fractions.

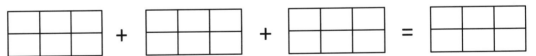

Equation

Shade the diagrams below to show two different fractions that add to 1. Then write an equation to show the sum of the fractions.

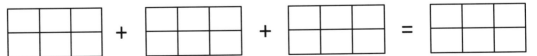

Equation

10 Shade the diagrams below to show three equal fractions that add to 1. Then write an equation to show the sum of the fractions.

Equation

Shade the diagrams below to show three different fractions that add to 1. Then write an equation to show the sum of the fractions.

Equation

11 Dominic ordered 1 whole pizza. Dominic ate $\frac{1}{5}$ of the pizza, Dominic's sister ate $\frac{1}{10}$ of the pizza, and Dominic's father ate $\frac{3}{10}$ of the pizza. What fraction of the pizza remains? Use the diagram below to help you find the answer.

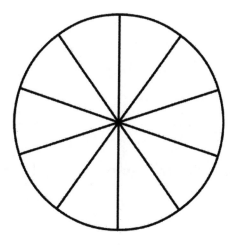

Answer _____ of the pizza remains

12 Tamara received some money for her birthday. She spent $\frac{1}{2}$ on a shirt, $\frac{1}{8}$ on a book, and $\frac{1}{4}$ on a bracelet. She saved the rest of the money. Divide the rectangle below into parts and shade the parts to show the fraction of the money she spent on each item. Use the diagram to find the fraction of the money she saved.

Answer _____ of the money saved

Quiz 29: Adding and Subtracting Mixed Numbers

1   What is the sum of $4\frac{2}{3}$ and $3\frac{2}{3}$?

    Ⓐ $7\frac{1}{3}$ Ⓑ $7\frac{2}{3}$ Ⓒ $8\frac{1}{3}$ Ⓓ $8\frac{2}{3}$

2   What is the difference of $3\frac{1}{6}$ and $1\frac{2}{6}$?

    Ⓐ $1\frac{3}{6}$ Ⓑ $1\frac{5}{6}$ Ⓒ $2\frac{3}{6}$ Ⓓ $2\frac{5}{6}$

3   Which fraction goes in the empty space to make the number sentence below true?

$$\frac{9}{4} + = 4$$

    Ⓐ $\frac{3}{4}$ Ⓑ $\frac{5}{4}$ Ⓒ $\frac{7}{4}$ Ⓓ $\frac{9}{4}$

4   Which sum is greater than 1?

    Ⓐ $\frac{1}{6} + \frac{1}{6} + \frac{1}{6}$ Ⓑ $\frac{2}{5} + \frac{2}{5} + \frac{2}{5}$

    Ⓒ $\frac{1}{10} + \frac{3}{10} + \frac{4}{10}$ Ⓓ $\frac{2}{8} + \frac{2}{8} + \frac{2}{8}$

5   Which sums below are equal to a whole number? Select all the correct answers.

    ☐ $1\frac{1}{6} + 2\frac{2}{6}$ ☐ $2\frac{4}{8} + 2\frac{2}{8}$ ☐ $1\frac{7}{8} + 1\frac{1}{8}$ ☐ $3\frac{1}{4} + 5\frac{3}{4}$

    ☐ $3\frac{1}{5} + 6\frac{5}{5}$ ☐ $5\frac{5}{6} + 1\frac{3}{6}$ ☐ $2\frac{3}{5} + 3\frac{2}{5}$ ☐ $1\frac{5}{10} + 2\frac{2}{10}$

6 Complete each problem in steps. In Step 1, convert the mixed numbers to improper fractions. In step 2, complete the calculation. In Step 3, write the improper fraction as a mixed number. The first one has been completed for you.

Problem	Step 1	Step 2	Step 3
$5\frac{2}{3} + 2\frac{2}{3}$	$\frac{17}{3} + \frac{8}{3}$	$\frac{25}{3}$	$8\frac{1}{3}$
$2\frac{3}{4} + 6\frac{3}{4}$			
$1\frac{5}{6} + 2\frac{2}{6}$			
$3\frac{3}{8} + 3\frac{4}{8}$			
$4\frac{7}{10} + 1\frac{6}{10}$			
$1\frac{78}{100} + 1\frac{35}{100}$			
$8\frac{1}{4} - 6\frac{2}{4}$			
$6\frac{1}{6} - 3\frac{2}{6}$			
$5\frac{2}{8} - 2\frac{7}{8}$			
$3\frac{4}{10} - 1\frac{5}{10}$			
$4\frac{3}{12} - 1\frac{8}{12}$			

7   Shade the diagram below to represent the sum of $2\frac{1}{4}$ and $1\frac{1}{2}$.

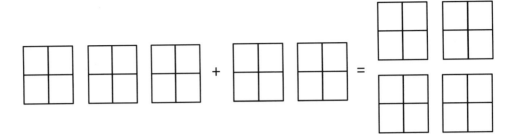

What is the sum of $2\frac{1}{4}$ and $1\frac{1}{2}$? _____

8   Shade the diagram below to represent the sum of $1\frac{7}{10}$ and $1\frac{9}{10}$.

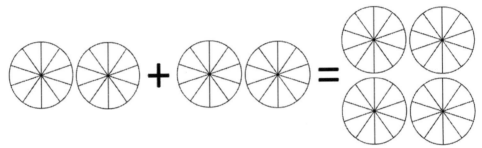

What is the sum of $1\frac{7}{10}$ and $1\frac{9}{10}$? _____

9   Use the number line below to find the sum of $1\frac{1}{3}$, $1\frac{2}{3}$, and $1\frac{2}{3}$. Then write the sum on the line below.

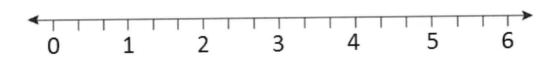

Answer _____

10 What is the sum of $3\frac{7}{12}$ and $4\frac{8}{12}$? Write the answer as a mixed number.

Show your work.

Answer _____

11 What is the value of $2\frac{4}{5} + 1\frac{2}{5} + 3\frac{3}{5}$? Write the answer as a mixed number.

Show your work.

Answer _____

12 What is the difference of $6\frac{3}{6}$ and $2\frac{4}{6}$? Write the answer as a mixed number.

Show your work.

Answer _____

13 What is the value of $5\frac{3}{8} - 1\frac{2}{8} - 2\frac{2}{8}$? Write the answer as a mixed number.

Show your work.

Answer _____

Quiz 30: Solving Word Problems Involving Fractions

1 Lana had a piece of timber $4\frac{1}{4}$ inches long. She cut off a section $2\frac{3}{4}$ inches long. What is the length of the remaining timber?

Ⓐ $1\frac{1}{2}$ inches   Ⓑ $1\frac{3}{4}$ inches   Ⓒ $2\frac{1}{4}$ inches   Ⓓ $2\frac{1}{2}$ inches

2 The diagram shows the length of two pieces of ribbon.

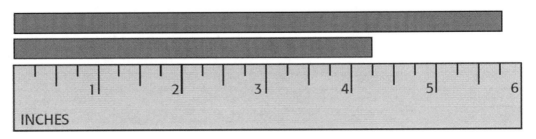

What is the difference in length between the two pieces of ribbon?

Ⓐ $\frac{3}{4}$ inches   Ⓑ $1\frac{1}{4}$ inches   Ⓒ $1\frac{1}{2}$ inches   Ⓓ $1\frac{3}{4}$ inches

3 Jeremy worked for $4\frac{5}{6}$ hours on Saturday and $3\frac{5}{6}$ hours on Sunday. How many hours did he work in all?

Ⓐ $7\frac{2}{6}$ hours   Ⓑ $7\frac{4}{6}$ hours   Ⓒ $8\frac{2}{6}$ hours   Ⓓ $8\frac{4}{6}$ hours

4 Cecilia has completed $3\frac{3}{10}$ miles of a 10-mile cycling race. Which of these are ways to find how many miles she has left to complete? Select all the correct answers.

☐ $10 - 3 - \frac{3}{10}$ ☐ $10 - \frac{9}{10}$ ☐ $10 - \frac{33}{10}$

☐ $\frac{10}{10} - \frac{33}{10}$ ☐ $\frac{100}{10} - \frac{33}{10}$ ☐ $10 - (3 \times \frac{3}{10})$

5 Write a subtraction equation that could be used to find the missing fraction, f, in the equation below. Then solve the equation to find the missing fraction.

$$2\frac{1}{8} + f = 4$$

Answer _____

6 Write an addition equation that could be used to find the missing fraction, f, in the equation below. Then solve the equation to find the missing fraction.

$$f - 1\frac{4}{6} = 2\frac{1}{6}$$

Answer _____

7 Bronwyn bought $3\frac{4}{8}$ pounds of peaches and $4\frac{3}{8}$ pounds of plums. Write an equation that can be used to find how many pounds of fruit she bought in all. Then solve the equation to find the answer.

Answer _____ pounds

8 Kirk is $4\frac{7}{12}$ feet tall. Hayley is $5\frac{1}{12}$ feet tall. Write an equation that can be used to find how much taller Hayley is than Kirk. Then solve the equation to find the answer.

Answer _____ feet

9   The table below shows how far four students traveled to school.

Student	Distance Traveled (miles)
Ahmed	$2\frac{4}{5}$
Bryce	$3\frac{1}{5}$
Dmitri	$4\frac{3}{5}$
Jared	$1\frac{2}{5}$

How much farther did Dmitri travel than Jared?

Show your work.

Answer _____ miles

How much farther did Dmitri travel than Ahmed?

Show your work.

Answer _____ miles

How much farther did Bryce travel than Jared?

Show your work.

Answer _____ miles

10 Jackie bought 3 supreme pizzas, 3 chicken pizzas, and 3 vegetarian pizzas for a party. The list below shows how much pizza of each type was eaten.

- $2\frac{7}{8}$ supreme pizzas

- $2\frac{3}{8}$ chicken pizzas

- $2\frac{1}{8}$ vegetarian pizzas

What fraction more of the supreme pizza was eaten than the vegetarian pizza?

Show your work.

Answer _____ pizzas

What fraction of the total pizza was eaten?

Show your work.

Answer _____ pizzas

What fraction of the total pizza remains?

Show your work.

Answer _____ pizzas

Quiz 31: Understanding Fractions and Multiplication

1   Which number makes the number sentence below true?

$$\frac{1}{6} \times \boxed{} = \frac{5}{6}$$

Ⓐ 3   Ⓑ 4   Ⓒ 5   Ⓓ 6

2   The fraction model below represents 6 whole units.

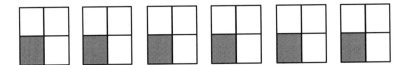

Which number sentence represents the amount of the fraction model that is shaded?

Ⓐ $4 \times \frac{1}{4}$ Ⓑ $4 \times \frac{1}{6}$ Ⓒ $6 \times \frac{1}{4}$ Ⓓ $6 \times \frac{1}{6}$

3   The fraction model below represents $4 \times \frac{3}{10}$.

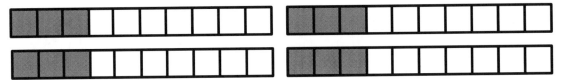

What is the value of $4 \times \frac{3}{10}$?

Ⓐ $\frac{7}{10}$ Ⓑ $\frac{12}{10}$ Ⓒ $\frac{3}{40}$ Ⓓ $\frac{12}{40}$

4   Which expression is the same as $\frac{1}{3} \times 4$?

Ⓐ $\frac{1}{3} + \frac{1}{3} + \frac{1}{3} + \frac{1}{3}$ Ⓑ $\frac{1}{3} \times \frac{4}{4}$ Ⓒ $\frac{1}{3} \times \frac{1}{4}$ Ⓓ $\frac{1}{3} + \frac{1}{3} + \frac{1}{3}$

5 Complete the missing number in each number sentence below.

$\dfrac{5}{4} = \underline{\hspace{1.5em}} \times \dfrac{1}{4}$ $\qquad\qquad$ $\dfrac{8}{5} = \underline{\hspace{1.5em}} \times \dfrac{1}{5}$

$\dfrac{7}{3} = \underline{\hspace{1.5em}} \times \dfrac{1}{3}$ $\qquad\qquad$ $\dfrac{4}{6} = \underline{\hspace{1.5em}} \times \dfrac{1}{6}$

$\dfrac{9}{10} = \underline{\hspace{1.5em}} \times \dfrac{1}{10}$ $\qquad\qquad$ $\dfrac{12}{8} = \underline{\hspace{1.5em}} \times \dfrac{1}{8}$

$\dfrac{11}{12} = \underline{\hspace{1.5em}} \times \dfrac{1}{12}$ $\qquad\qquad$ $\dfrac{31}{100} = \underline{\hspace{1.5em}} \times \dfrac{1}{100}$

6 Write each multiplication expression as an addition expression. Then complete the calculation to find the answer.

Multiplication Expression	Addition Expression	Answer
$\dfrac{1}{2} \times 4$		
$\dfrac{2}{3} \times 3$		
$\dfrac{2}{5} \times 4$		
$\dfrac{5}{6} \times 3$		
$\dfrac{3}{4} \times 5$		
$\dfrac{7}{8} \times 4$		

7   Use a whole number and a fraction to write a multiplication expression that is represented by the diagram below. Then solve the expression to find the answer.

Expression

Answer _____

8   Use a whole number and a fraction to write a multiplication expression that is represented by the diagram below. Then solve the expression to find the answer.

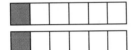 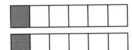 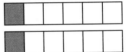 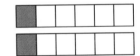

Expression

Answer _____

9   Shade the diagram below to represent the expression $\frac{1}{5} \times 6$.

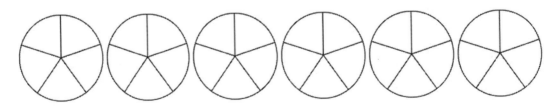

What is the value of $\frac{1}{5} \times 6$? _____

10   Shade the diagram below to represent the expression $\frac{1}{8} \times 4$.

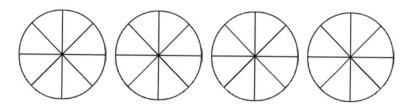

What is the value of $\frac{1}{8} \times 4$? _____

11   Write an equation that is represented by the diagram below.

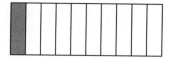 × 9 =

Equation

12   Shade the diagram below to show the product of $\frac{1}{5}$ and 4.

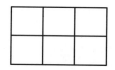 × 4 =

What is the product of $\frac{1}{5}$ and 4? _____

13   Shade the diagram below to show the product of $\frac{1}{6}$ and 7.

× 7 =

What is the product of $\frac{1}{6}$ and 7? _____

Quiz 32: Multiplying Fractions by Whole Numbers

1 What is the value of $\frac{2}{5} \times 3$?

    (A) $\frac{2}{15}$ (B) $\frac{6}{15}$ (C) $1\frac{1}{5}$ (D) $5\frac{1}{5}$

2 Which number makes the number sentence below true?

$$\frac{3}{12} \times \square = \frac{9}{12}$$

    (A) 3   (B) 4   (C) 6   (D) 9

3 Which expressions below are equal to whole numbers? Select all the correct answers.

    ☐ $\frac{2}{5} \times 4$ ☐ $\frac{1}{8} \times 16$ ☐ $\frac{2}{3} \times 6$

    ☐ $\frac{7}{10} \times 5$ ☐ $\frac{4}{12} \times 4$ ☐ $\frac{3}{4} \times 10$

    ☐ $\frac{6}{12} \times 8$ ☐ $\frac{1}{3} \times 9$ ☐ $\frac{3}{8} \times 6$

4 Shade the diagram below to show that $\frac{1}{4} \times 4 = \frac{1}{2} \times 2$.

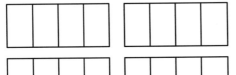
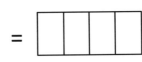

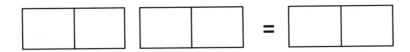

5 What is the value of x in the equation below?

$$\frac{1}{10} \times x = 5$$

Ⓐ 2 Ⓑ 20 Ⓒ 50 Ⓓ 100

6 Complete the missing number in each number sentence below.

$2 \times \frac{2}{6} = \underline{} \times \frac{1}{6}$ $5 \times \frac{3}{5} = \underline{} \times \frac{1}{5}$

$4 \times \frac{4}{8} = \underline{} \times \frac{2}{8}$ $6 \times \frac{3}{10} = \underline{} \times \frac{1}{10}$

$12 \times \frac{1}{6} = \underline{} \times \frac{3}{6}$ $4 \times \frac{1}{4} = \underline{} \times \frac{2}{4}$

$6 \times \frac{2}{5} = \underline{} \times \frac{4}{5}$ $10 \times \frac{8}{10} = \underline{} \times \frac{2}{10}$

7 Complete each multiplication below. Write the answer as an improper fraction and a mixed number.

Expression	Improper Fraction	Mixed Number
$4 \times \frac{4}{10}$		
$6 \times \frac{3}{5}$		
$7 \times \frac{2}{6}$		
$5 \times \frac{3}{12}$		
$8 \times \frac{7}{8}$		
$10 \times \frac{2}{3}$		

8   Use a whole number and a fraction to write an expression that is represented by the diagram below. Then solve the expression to find the answer. Write the answer as an improper fraction and a mixed number.

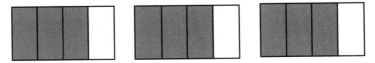

Expression _____

Answer _____ or _____

9   Use a whole number and a fraction to write an expression that is represented by the diagram below. Then solve the expression to find the answer. Write the answer as an improper fraction and a mixed number.

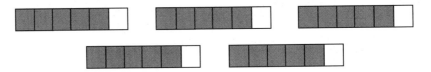

Expression _____

Answer _____ or _____

10   Shade the diagram below to represent the expression $\frac{3}{5} \times 6$.

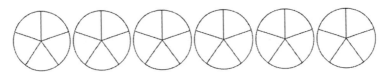

What is the value of $\frac{3}{5} \times 6$? Write your answer as an improper fraction and a mixed number.

Answer _____ or _____

11 Shade the diagram below to represent the expression $\frac{3}{8} \times 5$.

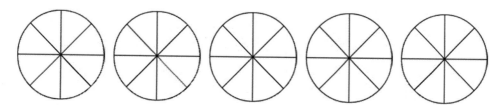

What is the value of $\frac{3}{8} \times 5$? Write your answer as an improper fraction and a mixed number.

Answer _____ or _____

12 Shade the diagram below to show the product of $\frac{2}{5}$ and 4.

× 4 =

What is the product of $\frac{2}{5}$ and 4? Write your answer as an improper fraction and a mixed number.

Answer _____ or _____

13 Shade the diagram below to show the product of $\frac{5}{6}$ and 7.

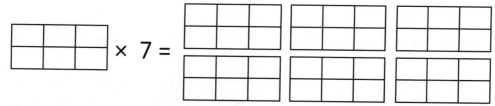

× 7 =

What is the product of $\frac{5}{6}$ and 7? Write your answer as an improper fraction and a mixed number.

Answer _____ or _____

Quiz 33: Solving Word Problems Involving Multiplying Fractions

1   Corey serves 12 glasses of orange juice. Each glass contains $\frac{1}{4}$ liter of juice. How many liters of orange juice does he serve in all?

    Ⓐ 2 liters   Ⓑ 3 liters   Ⓒ 4 liters   Ⓓ 6 liters

2   Sasha ran 8 laps of the school's running track. Each lap was $\frac{1}{3}$ of a mile. How far did Sasha run in all?

    Ⓐ 2 miles   Ⓑ $2\frac{2}{3}$ miles   Ⓒ 3 miles   Ⓓ $3\frac{1}{3}$ miles

3   Mario has blocks of timber measuring $2\frac{1}{6}$ feet each. He wants to place them in a row to make a path with a total length that is a whole number. How many blocks of timber could he place? Select all the possible answers.

    ☐ 6   ☐ 8   ☐ 10   ☐ 12

    ☐ 14   ☐ 15   ☐ 18   ☐ 20

    ☐ 22   ☐ 24   ☐ 26   ☐ 28

4   The books below each have a width of $\frac{7}{8}$ inches.

What is the total width of all the books?

    Ⓐ $4\frac{1}{8}$ inches   Ⓑ $4\frac{3}{8}$ inches   Ⓒ $4\frac{5}{8}$ inches   Ⓓ $4\frac{7}{8}$ inches

5 There were 4 students completing a mural. Each student completed $\frac{2}{10}$ of the mural. Shade the diagram below to show how much of the mural was completed in all.

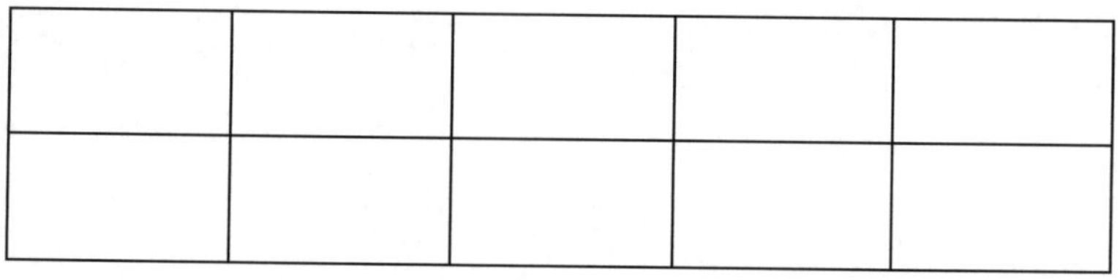

What fraction of the mural was completed in all? Write your answer in lowest form.

Answer _____

6 Morgan spends $\frac{5}{6}$ of an hour at the gym 5 days a week. Complete the diagram below to show how many hours Morgan spends at the gym each week.

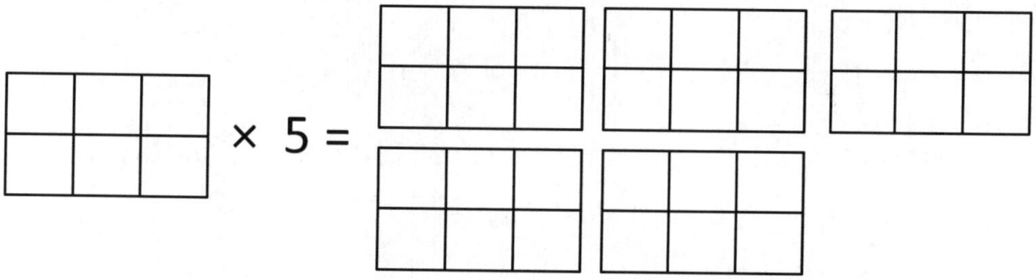

× 5 =

How many hours does Morgan spend at the gym each week? _____ hours

Explain how the diagram helped you find the answer.

_____

_____

_____

7 Dustin used 11 bricks to make a border along one edge of a garden bed. Each brick had a length of $\frac{11}{12}$ inches. What is the length of the edge of the garden bed? Write your answer as a mixed number.

Show your work.

Answer _____ inches

8 The list below shows how long four students practiced the violin in the month of March.

- Rebekah practiced for $\frac{3}{4}$ of an hour on 15 days.

- Carmen practiced for $\frac{5}{6}$ of an hour on 10 days.

- Allison practiced for $\frac{2}{3}$ of an hour on 12 days.

- Li practiced for $\frac{1}{2}$ of an hour on 18 days.

List the students in order from the student who practiced the least total time to the student who practiced the most total time.

Show your work.

Least total time   **Most total time**

_____   _____   _____   _____

9 Lenny is filling a fish tank with water. He fills a bowl with $\frac{3}{4}$ liters of water and pours it into the fish tank. He repeats this process a total of 9 times. How many liters of water would be in the fish tank in the end? Write your answer as a mixed number.

Show your work.

Answer _____ liters

10 A recipe for banana bread requires $1\frac{1}{2}$ cups of flour. Clare fills a $\frac{1}{2}$ cup measuring cup several times to measure out the flour. How many times will Clare need to fill the $\frac{1}{2}$ cup measuring cup to measure out $1\frac{1}{2}$ cups of flour? Show your work or explain how you found your answer.

Answer _____ times

Andy only has a measuring cup for $\frac{1}{4}$ cup. How many times will Andy need to fill the $\frac{1}{4}$ cup measuring cup to measure out $1\frac{1}{2}$ cups of flour? Show your work or explain how you found your answer.

Answer _____ times

Quiz 34: Understanding and Using Equivalent Decimal Fractions

1 Which fraction is equivalent to $\frac{7}{10}$?

(A) $\frac{70}{100}$　　　(B) $\frac{70}{10}$　　　(C) $\frac{7}{100}$　　　(D) $\frac{700}{100}$

2 Which fraction can be simplified to a fraction with a denominator of 10?

(A) $\frac{20}{100}$　　　(B) $\frac{54}{100}$　　　(C) $\frac{25}{100}$　　　(D) $\frac{33}{100}$

3 Which fraction is represented by the model below? Select all the correct answers.

☐ $\frac{1}{3}$　　　☐ $\frac{3}{10}$　　　☐ $\frac{30}{10}$　　　☐ $\frac{30}{100}$

4 What is the sum of $\frac{6}{100}$ and $\frac{2}{10}$?

(A) $\frac{8}{100}$　　　(B) $\frac{26}{100}$　　　(C) $\frac{62}{100}$　　　(D) $\frac{80}{100}$

5 Which fraction makes the equation below true?

$$\frac{5}{10} + \boxed{} = \frac{65}{100}$$

(A) $\frac{6}{100}$　　　(B) $\frac{13}{100}$　　　(C) $\frac{15}{100}$　　　(D) $\frac{60}{100}$

6   Rewrite each fraction as an equivalent fraction with a denominator of 100.

$$\frac{3}{10} = \qquad\qquad \frac{6}{10} = \qquad\qquad \frac{8}{10} = \qquad\qquad \frac{9}{10} =$$

7   Wade listed the six fractions below.

$$\frac{62}{100} \qquad \frac{6}{10} \qquad \frac{73}{100} \qquad \frac{78}{100} \qquad \frac{7}{10} \qquad \frac{69}{100}$$

Which fraction listed is the smallest? _____

Which fraction listed is the greatest? _____

Which two fractions listed have a difference of $\frac{1}{100}$? _____ and _____

8   For each addition problem below, convert both fractions to a fraction with a denominator of 100. Then add the two fractions to find the sum.

$$\frac{6}{10} + \frac{31}{100}$$

$$\frac{1}{10} + \frac{29}{100}$$

$$\frac{4}{10} + \frac{7}{100}$$

$$\frac{8}{10} + \frac{11}{100}$$

$$\frac{2}{10} + \frac{57}{100}$$

9 Each hundreds grid is shaded to represent a fraction. Shade the tens grid to represent an equivalent fraction. Then write the two shaded fractions on the blank lines.

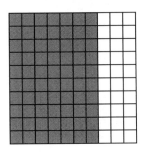 

Fractions _____ and _____

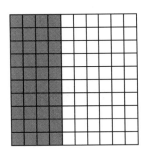 

Fractions _____ and _____

10 Shade the model below to represent the sum of $\frac{3}{10}$ and $\frac{27}{100}$. Then write the sum on the line below.

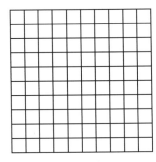

Sum _____

11   Trey is tiling his dining room floor. The fraction of the room he has tiled so far is represented by the shaded part of the diagram below. Trey tiles $\frac{2}{10}$ more of the dining room floor. What is the total amount tiled? Show your work or explain how you found your answer.

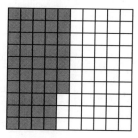

Answer _____

What fraction of the room remains to be tiled? Show your work or explain how you found your answer.

Answer _____

12   Phoebe states that the sum of $\frac{8}{10}$ and $\frac{9}{100}$ is $\frac{17}{100}$. Describe the mistake that Phoebe made when completing the calculation. Then write a number sentence that shows how to add the two fractions correctly.

_____

_____

Number sentence

Quiz 35: Expressing Fractions as Decimals

1   What is the value of $2\frac{7}{100}$ in decimal form?

     Ⓐ 0.27   Ⓑ 2.7   Ⓒ 2.07   Ⓓ 27.00

2   What is the value of $\frac{6}{10}$ in decimal form?

     Ⓐ 0.3   Ⓑ 0.03   Ⓒ 0.6   Ⓓ 0.06

3   Which decimal represents the shaded model below?

     Ⓐ 0.04   Ⓑ 0.08   Ⓒ 0.4   Ⓓ 0.8

4   Which shaded model represents 1.5?

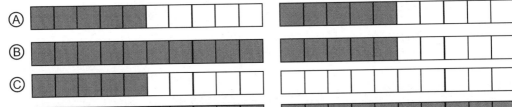

5   The model below is shaded to show $2\frac{40}{100}$.

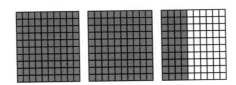

     Which decimal does the model represent?

     Ⓐ 2.4   Ⓑ 2.04   Ⓒ 200.4   Ⓓ 200.04

6   Which fractions are equivalent to 0.9? Select all the correct answers.

☐ $\frac{1}{9}$ ☐ $\frac{9}{10}$ ☐ $\frac{9}{100}$ ☐ $\frac{90}{100}$

☐ $\frac{9}{1}$ ☐ $\frac{10}{9}$ ☐ $\frac{100}{9}$ ☐ $\frac{10}{90}$

7   The model below is shaded to show $\frac{31}{100}$.

What decimal does the model represent?

Answer _____

8   The model below is shaded to show $1\frac{4}{10}$.

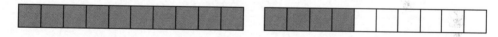

What is the value of $1\frac{4}{10}$ in decimal form?

Answer _____

9   Carly states that her bedroom is $9\frac{6}{10}$ meters long and $7\frac{3}{10}$ meters wide. Write the length and width of the bedroom in decimal form.

Answer _____ meters long and _____ meters wide

10　　Convert each fraction below to a fraction or a mixed number with a denominator of 10. Then convert the fraction to a decimal.

Fraction	Fraction with Denominator of 10	Decimal
$\dfrac{1}{2}$		
$\dfrac{1}{5}$		
$4\dfrac{3}{5}$		
$6\dfrac{4}{5}$		

11　　Convert each fraction below to a fraction or a mixed number with a denominator of 100. Then convert the fraction to a decimal.

Fraction	Fraction with Denominator of 100	Decimal
$\dfrac{9}{20}$		
$\dfrac{3}{4}$		
$\dfrac{23}{25}$		
$\dfrac{11}{50}$		
$5\dfrac{13}{20}$		

12   Plot the fractions listed below on the number line.

$$\frac{3}{10}, \frac{9}{10}, 1\frac{1}{10}, 1\frac{7}{10}$$

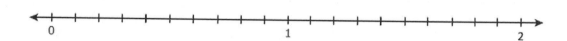

Write the decimal that is equivalent to each fraction.

$\frac{3}{10} =$ $\frac{9}{10} =$ $1\frac{1}{10} =$ $1\frac{7}{10} =$

13   Plot the decimals listed below on the number line.

0.4, 0.8, 1.2, 1.6

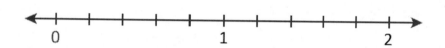

Write the fraction that is equivalent to each decimal. Write each fraction in lowest terms.

0.4 =   0.8 =   1.2 =   1.6 =

14   Victoria's best time for a 100-meter race is $13\frac{73}{100}$ seconds. Anna's best time is $13\frac{6}{10}$ seconds. Convert Victoria's and Anna's best times to decimals. Write your answers on the lines below.

Victoria _____ seconds   **Anna** _____ seconds

Quiz 36: Comparing Decimals

1   Which number is greater than 0.75?

    Ⓐ 0.68   Ⓑ 0.72   Ⓒ 0.79   Ⓓ 0.57

2   The two models below represent two decimals.

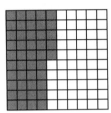 

    Which of the following compares the two decimals?

    Ⓐ 0.45 > 0.52   Ⓑ 0.45 < 0.52   Ⓒ 4.5 > 5.2   Ⓓ 4.5 < 5.2

3   Michael made the table below to show how much he received in tips on the four days that he worked.

Day	Amount
Monday	$31.55
Tuesday	$31.81
Thursday	$31.75
Friday	$31.09

    On which day did Michael earn the most in tips?

    Ⓐ Monday   Ⓑ Tuesday   Ⓒ Thursday   Ⓓ Friday

4   Ronald competed in a swimming race. All the students finished the race in between 45.8 seconds and 47.6 seconds. Which of the following could have been Ronald's time? Select all the possible answers.

    ☐ 45.97   ☐ 45.38   ☐ 47.75   ☐ 47.12

    ☐ 45.09   ☐ 47.95   ☐ 45.82   ☐ 47.55

5   Shade the models below to compare the two decimals. Then write <, >, or = in the empty box to show how the two decimals compare.

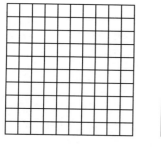 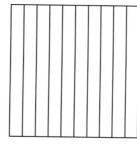 

0.15   0.2

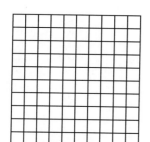 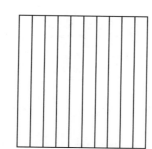 

0.04   0.4

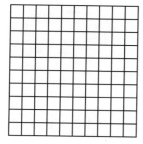 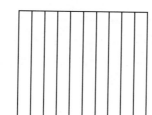 

0.62   0.6

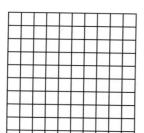 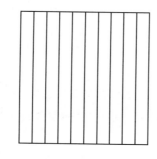

0.80   0.8

6   Each model below represents one whole. Shade sections of each model to represent 0.3, 0.8, 0.1, and 0.5. Then write the decimals in the correct places in the number sentence.

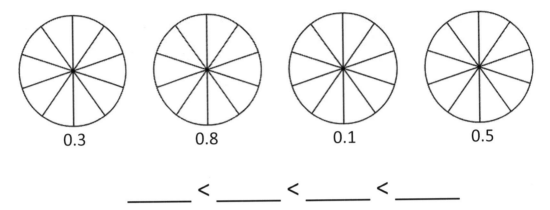

0.3   0.8   0.1   0.5

_____ < _____ < _____ < _____

7   Place the symbol <, >, or = in the empty box to make each number sentence correct.

4.15 ☐ 4.51   3.06 ☐ 3.60   2.13 ☐ 2.17

5.90 ☐ 5.9   7.58 ☐ 7.38   9.94 ☐ 9.56

8   The table shows the amount of rainfall for the first five days of the week.

Day	Monday	Tuesday	Wednesday	Thursday	Friday
Rainfall (cm)	3.58	3.18	3.09	3.62	3.37

What was the lowest rainfall over the 5 days? _____ cm

What was the highest rainfall over the 5 days? _____ cm

On Saturday, the rainfall was between the rainfall on Monday and Thursday.

Write two possible rainfalls for Saturday. _____ cm or _____ cm

9   Plot the decimals 0.2, 0.27, 0.14, 0.38 and 0.33 on the number line below.

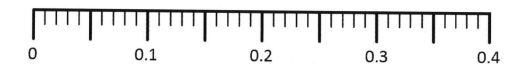

Use the number line to compare the pairs of decimals below. Place the symbol <, >, or = in the empty box to make each number sentence correct.

0.2 ☐ 0.27   0.2 ☐ 0.14   0.38 ☐ 0.33

10   Plot the decimals 0.7, 1.1, and 1.6 on the number line below.

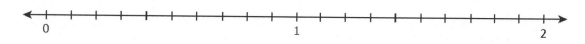

Use the number line to list three decimals more than 0.7 but less than 1.1.

_____, _____, and _____

Use the number line to list three decimals more than 1.6 but less than 2.

_____, _____, and _____

11   Calie wrote the number sentence below and stated that 8.05 is greater than 8.4 because 5 is greater than 4.

$$8.05 > 8.4$$

Describe the mistake that Calie made.

_____

_____

Quizzes 37 to 50

Measurement and Data

Directions

Read each question carefully. For each multiple-choice question, fill in the circle for the correct answer. For other types of questions, follow the directions given in the question.

You may use a ruler and a protractor to help you answer questions. You should answer the questions without using a calculator.

MATHEMATICS SKILLS LIST
For Parents, Teachers, and Tutors

Quizzes 37 through 50 cover these skills from the Georgia Standards of Excellence.

Measurement and Data

Solve problems involving measurement and conversion of measurements from a larger unit to a smaller unit.

1. Know relative sizes of measurement units within one system of units including km, m, cm; kg, g; lb, oz.; l, ml; hr, min, sec.
    a. Understand the relationship between gallons, cups, quarts, and pints.
    b. Express larger units in terms of smaller units within the same measurement system.
    c. Record measurement equivalents in a two column table.
2. Use the four operations to solve word problems involving distances, intervals of time, liquid volumes, masses of objects, and money, including problems involving simple fractions or decimals, and problems that require expressing measurements given in a larger unit in terms of a smaller unit. Represent measurement quantities using diagrams such as number line diagrams that feature a measurement scale.
3. Apply the area and perimeter formulas for rectangles in real world and mathematical problems.

Represent and interpret data.

4. Make a line plot to display a data set of measurements in fractions of a unit (1/2, 1/4, 1/8). Solve problems involving addition and subtraction of fractions with common denominators by using information presented in line plots.

Geometric measurement: understand concepts of angle and measure angles.

5. Recognize angles as geometric shapes that are formed wherever two rays share a common endpoint, and understand concepts of angle measurement.
    a. An angle is measured with reference to a circle with its center at the common endpoint of the rays, by considering the fraction of the circular arc between the points where the two rays intersect the circle. An angle that turns through 1/360 of a circle is called a "one-degree angle," and can be used to measure angles.
    b. An angle that turns through n one-degree angles is said to have an angle measure of n degrees.
6. Measure angles in whole-number degrees using a protractor. Sketch angles of specified measure.
7. Recognize angle measure as additive. When an angle is decomposed into non-overlapping parts, the angle measure of the whole is the sum of the angle measures of the parts. Solve addition and subtraction problems to find unknown angles on a diagram in real world and mathematical problems.

8. Recognize area as additive. Find areas of rectilinear figures by decomposing them into non-overlapping rectangles and adding the areas of the non-overlapping parts, applying this technique to solve real world problems.

Quiz 37: Comparing Units

1   A bike race traveled from end of a town to the other. What was the most likely distance of the bike race?

     Ⓐ 40 millimeters   Ⓑ 40 centimeters

     Ⓒ 40 kilometers   Ⓓ 40 meters

2   Which of these is most likely to be the length of a cob of corn?

     Ⓐ 7 feet   Ⓑ 7 inches   Ⓒ 7 yards   Ⓓ 7 miles

3   Which is the best estimate of the mass of a truck?

     Ⓐ 5 tons   Ⓑ 5 pounds   Ⓒ 50 ounces   Ⓓ 50 kilograms

4   Justin makes a cup of herb tea by adding hot water to a tea cup.

     About how much water could Justin have added to the tea cup?

     Ⓐ 200 milliliters   Ⓑ 200 pints   Ⓒ 200 liters   Ⓓ 200 quarts

5   Which measurement is the smallest?

     Ⓐ 1 meter   Ⓑ 1 centimeter   Ⓒ 1 millimeter   Ⓓ 1 kilometer

6   Order the amounts below from the smallest amount to the greatest amount. Write the numbers 1, 2, 3, 4 on the lines to show the order.

_____ 1 quart   _____ 1 gallon   _____ 1 pint   _____ 1 cup

7   For a school project, the students found the mass of items in a kitchen. For each item listed below, select the correct unit of either grams or kilograms. Write kg or g on the blank line to show your choice.

Item	Mass
fridge	85 ____
wooden spoon	40 ____
microwave oven	26 ____
dinner plate	455 ____
teaspoon	22 ____
cheese grater	140 ____
blender	16 ____

8   Which of these measurements are about 1 foot? Select all the correct answers.

☐ the width of a laptop computer

☐ the length of a computer mouse

☐ the height of a computer desk

☐ the length of a keyboard

☐ the width of a business card

☐ the height of a filing cabinet

9 A list of food items are given below. The items can be sorted by mass. Estimate the mass of each item and place it in the correct place in the table. Complete the table so that there are 4 items in each category.

grain of rice	apple	banana	peanut
pumpkin	watermelon	bean	egg
pineapple	French fry	loaf of bread	turkey

Estimated Mass of Items

Less than 10 grams	Between 11 and 1000 grams	Over 1 kilogram

10 A list of distances is shown below.

30 cm   305 mm   3 m   34 cm   330 cm

Place the measurements listed in order from the smallest distance to the greatest distance. Show your work or explain how you found your answer.

Smallest   **Greatest**

_____   _____   _____   _____   _____

11 Harriet fills the blender below to the top to make a smoothie.

Which of these is the most likely total volume of smoothie made? Circle the most likely answer.

3 gallons   3 quarts   3 pints   3 cups

Harriett pours all the liquid from the blender into 6 glasses. She pours an equal amount into each glass. Which of these is the most likely amount of smoothie in each glass? Circle the most likely answer.

1 gallon   1 quart   1 pint   1 cup

Explain how you chose the answer above.

_____

_____

_____

12 Jamie held his breath for 1 minute. Kara held her breath for 70 seconds. Who held their breath for the longest? Show your work or explain how you found your answer.

Answer _____

Quiz 38: Converting Units of Measurement

1   Alison bought a half gallon carton of milk. How many quarts of milk did the milk carton contain?

Ⓐ 1 quart   Ⓑ 2 quarts   Ⓒ 4 quarts   Ⓓ 8 quarts

2   Mrs. Masters added 2 liters of oil to her car. How many milliliters of oil did Mrs. Masters use?

Ⓐ 20 mL   Ⓑ 200 mL   Ⓒ 2,000 mL   Ⓓ 20,000 mL

$2 \times 1,000 = 2,000$

3   Which of the following is equal to 10 hours?

Ⓐ 600 minutes   Ⓑ 1,000 minutes

Ⓒ 10,000 seconds   Ⓓ 60,000 seconds

4   Marcus competed in a marathon. He ran 42 kilometers. How many meters did Marcus run?

Ⓐ 420 m   Ⓑ 4,200 m   Ⓒ 42,000 m   Ⓓ 420,000 m

$42 \times 1,000 = 42,000$

5   A pumpkin has a mass of 4 pounds. Which pumpkins below have a mass greater than 4 pounds? Select all the correct answers.

☑ 48 ounces   ☐ 52 ounces   ☐ 60 ounces

☐ 58 ounces   ☑ 80 ounces   ☑ 66 ounces

☐ 42 ounces   ☑ 86 ounces   ☐ 50 ounces

$4 \times 16 = 64$

6   Bananas weigh between 3 and 5 ounces each. Donna bought 1 pound of bananas. About how many bananas did Donna buy?

Ⓐ 2 bananas   Ⓑ 4 bananas   Ⓒ 48 bananas   Ⓓ 64 bananas

7   A list of heights is shown below.

2 yards   7 feet   48 inches   5 feet   88 inches

Place the heights listed in order from the shortest to the tallest. Show your work or explain how you found your answer.

Shortest   **Tallest**

_____   _____   _____   _____   _____

8   The table shows the relationship between gallons, quarts, and pints. Complete the table with the missing measurements.

Gallons	Quarts	Pints
	4	
		16
4		
	32	
		80

9 The width of a field is 180 feet. What is the width of the field in yards? What is the width of the field in inches?

Show your work.

Answer _____ yards or _____ inches

10 Kendra squeezed some oranges and collected 4 pints of orange juice. How many quarts of orange juice did she collect?

Show your work.

Answer _____ quarts

11 It took Bianca 3 hours and 10 minutes to travel to her aunt's house. How long did the trip take in minutes?

Show your work.

Answer _____ minutes

12 A puppy weighed 6 kilograms at the start of the week. It's weight increased by 280 grams by the end of the week. How much did the puppy weigh at the end of the week?

Show your work.

Answer _____ grams

13   The diameter of a basketball is 24 cm. The diameter of a baseball is 75 mm.

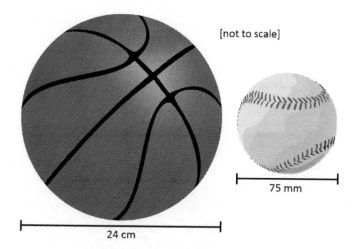

[not to scale]

75 mm

24 cm

What is the difference between the diameter of the basketball and the diameter of the baseball?

Show your work.

Answer _____ millimeters

14   There are 5,280 feet in a mile. Jackson wants to walk 2 miles. He has already walked 8,500 feet. How many more feet does he need to walk to reach 2 miles?

Show your work.

Answer _____ feet

Quiz 39: Solving Measurement Word Problems

1 Ariel's car weighs 2 tons. Derek's car weighs 2,480 pounds. What is the difference between the weights of the two cars?

Ⓐ 480 pounds   Ⓑ 720 pounds

Ⓒ 1,520 pounds   Ⓓ 2,478 pounds

2 The clock below shows the time in the afternoon that Edwin got on a train.

Edwin got off the train $1\frac{3}{4}$ hours later. What time did Edwin get off the train?

Ⓐ 3:10 p.m.   Ⓑ 3:40 p.m.   Ⓒ 4:10 p.m.   Ⓓ 4:40 p.m.

3 Janelle drove at 55 miles per hour for 4 hours, and then 40 miles per hour for $2\frac{1}{2}$ hours. How far did she drive in all?

Ⓐ 240 miles   Ⓑ 300 miles   Ⓒ 320 miles   Ⓓ 340 miles

4 The scale shows the mass of 9 packets of peanuts.

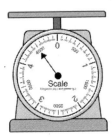

If each packet has the same mass, what is the mass of each packet?

Answer _____ grams

5   George is mixing paint. He needs to add $\frac{1}{4}$ liter of yellow paint to every liter of blue paint. How many liters of yellow paint does he need to add to 20 liters of blue paint?

Show your work.

Answer _____ liters

6   Melinda has 24 quarts of lemonade. She wants to pour it into glasses that hold 3 pints each. How many glasses can she fill?

Show your work.

Answer _____ glasses

7   The diagram shows how much milk and cream Ky uses to make custard.

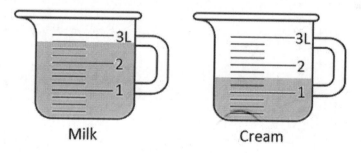

Milk   Cream

How much milk and cream does he use in all?

Show your work.

Answer _____ liters

8   The clocks below show the time that football practice starts and finishes.

Start   Finish

The coach wants to divide the football practice into 4 sessions of equal length. How many minutes should each session be?

Show your work.

Answer _____ minutes

9   Three 1-liter jugs are filled with orange juice to the lines shown below.

How many cups of 100 mL each could be filled with all the orange juice?

Show your work.

Answer _____ cups

10 Stefan made a path by laying down planks of wood, as shown below.

Each plank of wood was $2\frac{1}{2}$ feet long and $\frac{1}{2}$ foot wide. He left a gap of 1 inch between the planks. What is the total length of the path, in inches?

Show your work.

Answer _____ inches

What is the total width of the path, in inches?

Show your work.

Answer _____ inches

11 It costs 5 quarters to do one load of washing. How much would it cost, in dollars, to do 4 loads of washing? Show your work or explain how you found your answer.

Answer $_____

Quiz 40: Representing Measurement Problems

1 Jackie needs $\frac{1}{2}$ cup of honey for a recipe. She measures it out by filling a $\frac{1}{8}$ cup measuring cup several times. Which expression shows how many times she will need to fill the measuring cup?

Ⓐ $\frac{1}{2} \div \frac{1}{8}$ Ⓑ $\frac{1}{2} - \frac{1}{8}$ Ⓒ $\frac{1}{2} + \frac{1}{8}$ Ⓓ $\frac{1}{2} \times \frac{1}{8}$

2 The hundreds grid below represents 1 meter. What does the shaded area of the grid represent?

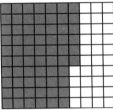

Ⓐ 66 mm   Ⓑ 66 m   Ⓒ 66 km   Ⓓ 66 cm

3 The diagram below represents the lengths of yards and feet.

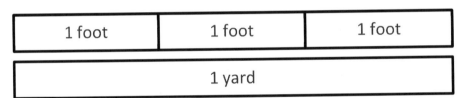

| 1 foot | 1 foot | 1 foot |

| 1 yard |

Which measurement in feet is equal to 30 yards? Write and solve an equation to show your answer.

Equation

Answer _____ feet

Which measurement in yards is equal to 18 feet? Write and solve an equation to show your answer.

Equation

Answer _____ yards

4 There are 36 inches in 1 yard. Shade the diagram below to represent $\frac{1}{6}$ yards.

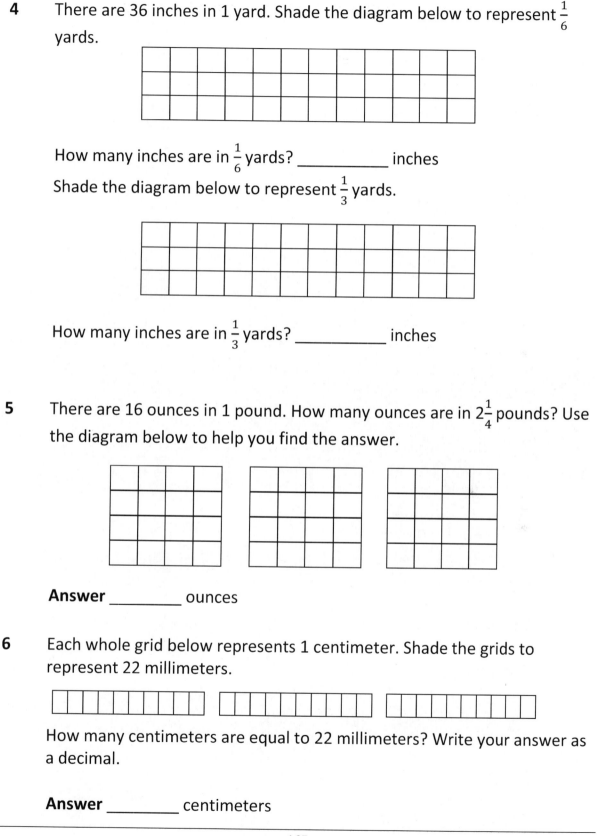

How many inches are in $\frac{1}{6}$ yards? _____ inches

Shade the diagram below to represent $\frac{1}{3}$ yards.

How many inches are in $\frac{1}{3}$ yards? _____ inches

5 There are 16 ounces in 1 pound. How many ounces are in $2\frac{1}{4}$ pounds? Use the diagram below to help you find the answer.

Answer _____ ounces

6 Each whole grid below represents 1 centimeter. Shade the grids to represent 22 millimeters.

How many centimeters are equal to 22 millimeters? Write your answer as a decimal.

Answer _____ centimeters

7 Anna is 59 inches tall. Anna is 2.5 inches shorter than Corey. Corey is 3.5 inches taller than Morgan. Use the number line below to show the heights of Anna, Corey, and Morgan. Then write the heights on the lines below.

Corey is _____ inches tall.

Morgan is _____ inches tall.

8 The fine for having a library book overdue is a basic fee of $3 plus an additional $0.50 for each day that the book is overdue. Use the number line below to find the total fine for having a book overdue for 7 days. Then write the total fine below.

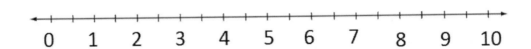

Answer $_____

9 Colin started work at 1:15 p.m. He worked until 3:45 p.m. On the number line, plot the points to show when Colin started and finished work.

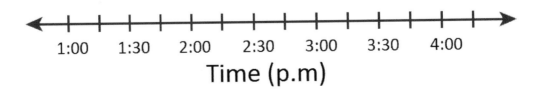

How long did Colin work for? _____ hours, _____ minutes

10   A bus leaves a stop every 45 minutes. The first bus leaves at 6:15 p.m. Plot the times that each bus leaves between 6 and 10 p.m.

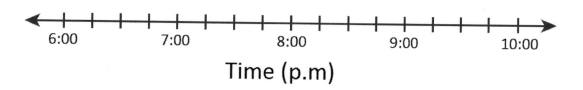

Time (p.m)

Wayne arrives at the bus stop at 7:30 p.m. How long will he have to wait for the next bus? _____ minutes

Samantha arrives at the bus stop at 8:55 p.m. How long will she have to wait for the next bus? _____ minutes

11   The cooking time for a roast is $\frac{1}{3}$ hour for every 500 grams. Find the cooking time for a small roast weighing 3500 grams and a large roast weighing 5500 grams. Plot the cooking time for the small and large roasts on the number line below.

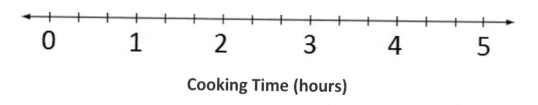

Cooking Time (hours)

How much longer does the large roast take to cook than the small roast? Show your work or explain how you found your answer.

Answer _____ hours

Quiz 41: Solving Area Problems

1 A rectangular dining room is 9 feet wide and 12 feet long. What is the area of the dining room?

Ⓐ 42 sq. ft   Ⓑ 84 sq. ft   Ⓒ 96 sq. ft   Ⓓ 108 sq. ft

2 The rectangle below has an area of 36 square centimeters.

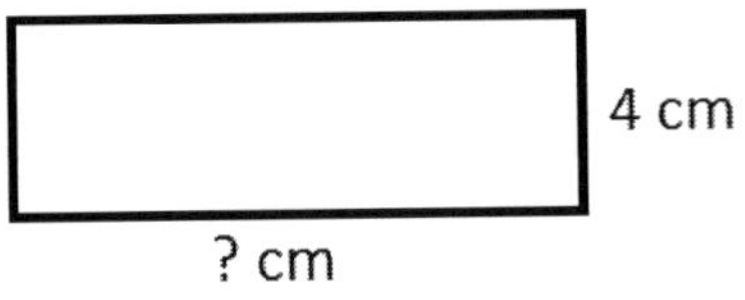

4 cm

? cm

What is the length of the rectangle?

Ⓐ 8 cm   Ⓑ 9 cm   Ⓒ 12 cm   Ⓓ 14 cm

3 Complete the equation that can be used to find the area of the shaded part of the design, in square units. Then write the area on the line.

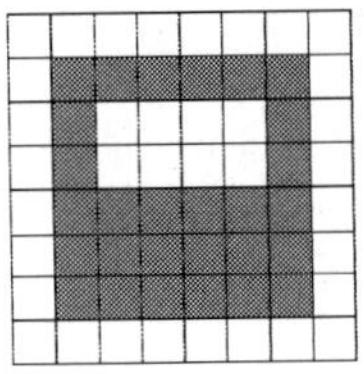

Equation (___ × ___) - (___ × ___) = _____   **Area** _____ square units

4 What is the area of the rectangle shown below?

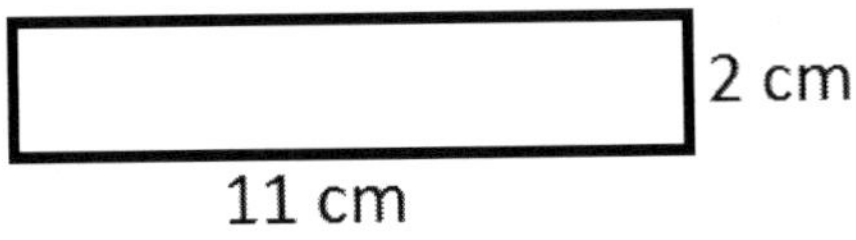

2 cm

11 cm

Answer _____ cm^2

5 Courtney wants to make a garden with an area of 240 square feet. Select all the possible dimensions of the garden.

☐ 24 feet by 10 feet   ☐ 40 feet by 80 feet   ☐ 8 feet by 30 feet

☐ 6 feet by 20 feet   ☐ 48 by 5 feet   ☐ 100 feet by 20 feet

6   The table shows how the area of a rectangle with a fixed width changes as the height changes.

Height (inches)	Area (square inches)
2	6
4	12
6	18
9	27

What is the width of the rectangle? _____ inches

Write four equations that show that the width is the same for all the rectangles.

7   Calvin has rectangular paddocks on his farm with areas of 640 square meters. The lengths and widths of the paddocks are whole numbers. Complete the missing number in each equation to find the possible pairs of dimensions.

$$20 \times \underline{\hspace{1cm}} = 640 \qquad 80 \times \underline{\hspace{1cm}} = 640$$

$$64 \times \underline{\hspace{1cm}} = 640 \qquad 16 \times \underline{\hspace{1cm}} = 640$$

Find two other possible pairs of dimensions for the paddocks. Show or explain how you found your answer.

Answer _____ by _____ meters or _____ by _____ meters

8   The grids below have squares with units of 1 square centimeter (cm²). Draw a rectangle on each grid to match the information given, and complete the missing information.

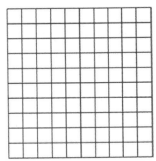   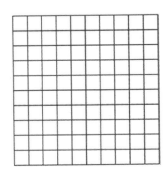   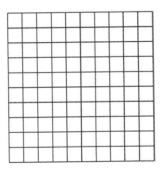

Length = 5 cm   Length = 7 cm   Length = _____ cm
Height = 9 cm   Height = _____ cm   Height = 6 cm
Area = _____ cm²   Area = 56 cm²   Area = 18 cm²

9   Mr. Connor is planning to put solar panels on his roof. Each panel has the dimensions shown below.

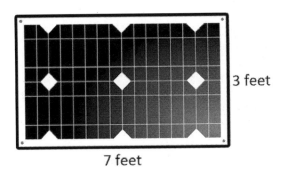

3 feet

7 feet

He wants the solar panels to have a total area of at least 150 square feet. How many solar panels should he place? What will be the total area of the solar panels?

Show your work.

Answer _____ solar panels, total area of _____ square feet

10   Leah is making rectangular picture frames. She wants each picture frame to be as below.

- The length and width will be in whole inches.
- The length will be greater than the width.
- The length will be less than 20 inches.
- The area will be 48 square inches.

On the grid below, draw three possible rectangles that represent the shape of the picture frames. Then write the length, width, and area of each picture frame below.

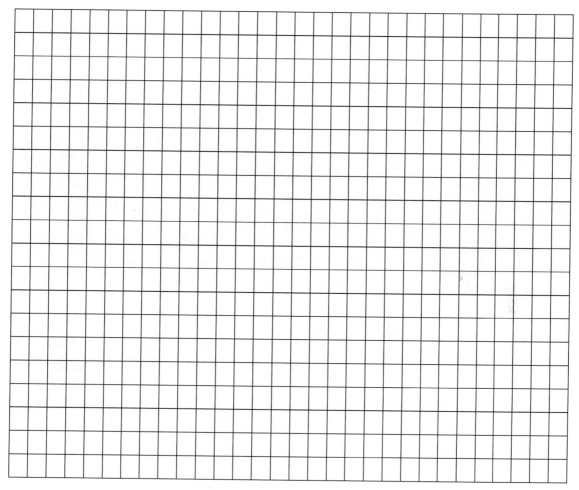

1.   length _____ in.   width _____ in.   area _____ in.²

2.   length _____ in.   width _____ in.   area _____ in.²

3.   length _____ in.   width _____ in.   area _____ in.²

Quiz 42: Solving Perimeter Problems

1   A rectangular cutting board is 16 inches long and 11 inches wide. What is the perimeter of the cutting board?

    Ⓐ 27 inches   Ⓑ 54 inches   Ⓒ 108 inches   Ⓓ 176 inches

2   Which expression can be used to find the perimeter of a rectangle with a length of 6 meters and a width of 18 meters, in meters?

    Ⓐ 6 + 18   Ⓑ 6 × 18

    Ⓒ 2 × (6 + 18)   Ⓓ 18 + 18 + 18 + 6 + 6 + 6

3   Which of these could be the perimeter of a square with whole-number side lengths?

    Ⓐ 25 inches   Ⓑ 29 inches   Ⓒ 34 inches   Ⓓ 48 inches

4   Which rectangles have a perimeter the same as the rectangle shown below? Select all the correct answers.

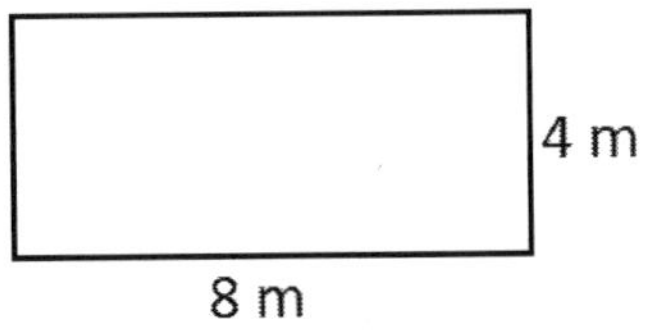

    ☐ 16 cm by 2 cm   ☐ 7 cm by 5 cm   ☐ 3 cm by 9 cm

    ☐ 10 cm by 3 cm   ☐ 16 cm by 1 cm   ☐ 14 cm by 6 cm

5   The rectangle below has a perimeter of 36 centimeters.

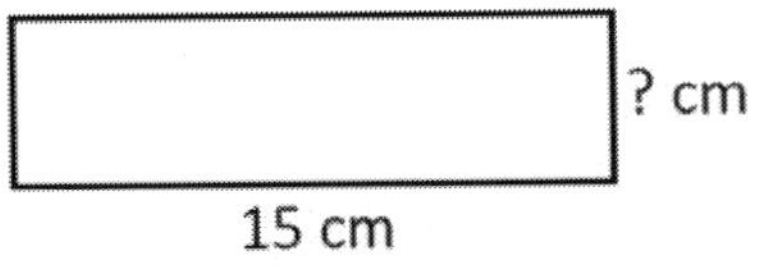

What is the width of the rectangle?

Answer _____ cm

6 The table below shows the length, width, and perimeter of different rectangular fields. Complete the table with the missing information.

Length (meters)	Width (meters)	Perimeter (meters)
20	12	
	18	84
15		62
	6	38
14	53	
	25	200
50		124

7 The shaded area on the grid shows a rectangle with a perimeter of 16 units. Draw a rectangle on the second and third grids with different dimensions but the same perimeter.

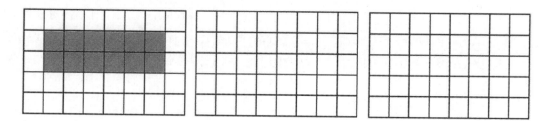

Complete the equations to show that the perimeters are the same.

Grid 1   2 × (___ + ___) = ___   or   ___ + ___ + ___ + ___ = ___

Grid 2   2 × (___ + ___) = ___   or   ___ + ___ + ___ + ___ = ___

Grid 3   2 × (___ + ___) = ___   or   ___ + ___ + ___ + ___ = ___

8   The diagram below shows the dimensions of a school's stage.

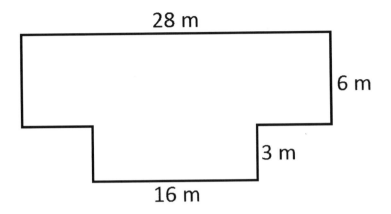

What is the perimeter of the stage? Show your work or explain how you found your answer.

Answer _____ meters

9   Juliet is making a rectangular poster that is 20 inches long and 45 inches high. She wants to place ribbon around all the edges of the poster with no ribbon overlapping. The ribbon comes in rolls of 25 inches each. How many rolls will she need to buy? How much ribbon will be left over? Show your work or explain how you found your answer.

Answer _____ rolls of ribbon, _____ inches of ribbon left over

10   Janice is planning to make a rectangular sandpit. She wants the sandpit to be as below.

- The length and width will be in whole feet.
- The length will be greater than the width.
- It will use 18 feet of logs as the border.

On the grid below, draw four rectangles that represent possible dimensions of the sandpit.

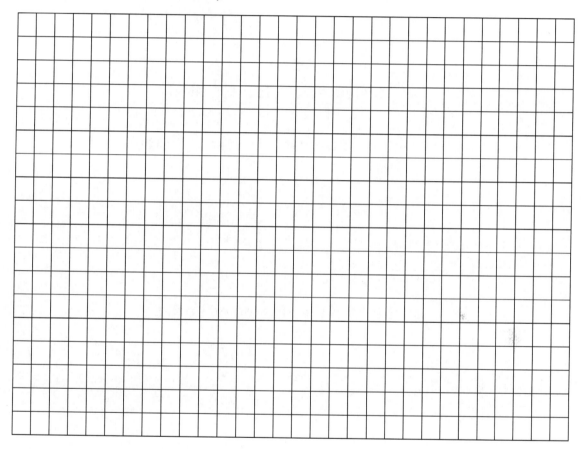

Janice wants to use the set of dimensions that gives the sandpit the greatest area. Which set of dimensions should she choose? Show your work or explain your answer.

Answer _____ by _____ feet

Quiz 43: Displaying Measurement Data in Line Plots

1   Cameron asked the students in his class who walk to school how far they live from school. He represented the data in the line plot below.

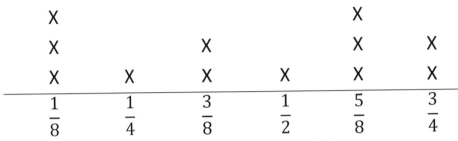

Distance from School (miles)

How many students does the data in the line plot represent?

Ⓐ 6   Ⓑ 8   Ⓒ 10   Ⓓ 12

2   The list shows the height of the bar that students cleared in a high jump competition.

Height of the Bar Cleared (inches)

$$3, 2\frac{1}{2}, 2\frac{1}{2}, 2, 2, 2\frac{1}{2}, 2\frac{1}{4}, 2\frac{1}{2}, 1\frac{3}{4}, 2\frac{3}{4}, 2, 2\frac{1}{2}, 1\frac{3}{4}$$

Use the data to complete the line plot below.

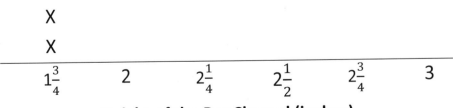

Height of the Bar Cleared (inches)

3   The table shows the mass of ten kittens when they were born.

Mass of Kittens (ounces)

Kitten 1	$3\frac{1}{2}$
Kitten 2	$3\frac{1}{8}$
Kitten 3	$3\frac{1}{4}$
Kitten 4	$3\frac{3}{4}$
Kitten 5	$3\frac{1}{2}$
Kitten 6	$3\frac{3}{8}$
Kitten 7	$3\frac{3}{8}$
Kitten 8	$3\frac{1}{8}$
Kitten 9	$3\frac{5}{8}$
Kitten 10	$3\frac{3}{4}$

Use the data in the table to complete the line plot below.

$3\frac{1}{8}$ $3\frac{1}{4}$ $3\frac{3}{8}$ $3\frac{1}{2}$ $3\frac{5}{8}$ $3\frac{3}{4}$

Mass of Kittens (ounces)

4 Holly measured the amount of rainfall on the first 14 rainy days in winter. The data is shown in the table below.

Amount of Daily Rainfall (inches)

Day 1	$2\frac{1}{2}$	Day 8	2
Day 2	$2\frac{1}{4}$	Day 9	$1\frac{3}{4}$
Day 3	$2\frac{1}{4}$	Day 10	$2\frac{1}{2}$
Day 4	$1\frac{3}{4}$	Day 11	$2\frac{1}{4}$
Day 5	$2\frac{1}{4}$	Day 12	$1\frac{3}{4}$
Day 6	$2\frac{3}{4}$	Day 13	$1\frac{1}{2}$
Day 7	$2\frac{3}{4}$	Day 14	$2\frac{3}{4}$

Use the data in the table to complete the line plot below.

$$1\frac{1}{2} \qquad 1\frac{3}{4} \qquad 2 \qquad 2\frac{1}{4} \qquad 2\frac{1}{2} \qquad 2\frac{3}{4} \qquad 3$$

Amount of Daily Rainfall (inches)

On how many rainy days did 2 inches or more of rain fall? _____ days

Which amount of rainfall was most common? _____ inches

5   Jordan measured the height of 20 corn plants in a field. The data she collected is shown below.

Height of Plants (feet)

Plant 1	$4\frac{7}{8}$	Plant 11	$4\frac{3}{4}$
Plant 2	$4\frac{5}{8}$	Plant 12	4
Plant 3	$4\frac{1}{4}$	Plant 13	$4\frac{1}{4}$
Plant 4	$4\frac{3}{4}$	Plant 14	$4\frac{1}{2}$
Plant 5	$4\frac{1}{8}$	Plant 15	$4\frac{1}{4}$
Plant 6	$4\frac{3}{8}$	Plant 16	$4\frac{3}{4}$
Plant 7	$4\frac{3}{4}$	Plant 17	$4\frac{7}{8}$
Plant 8	4	Plant 18	$4\frac{5}{8}$
Plant 9	$4\frac{1}{4}$	Plant 19	5
Plant 10	$4\frac{1}{8}$	Plant 20	$4\frac{5}{8}$

Use the data in the table to complete the line plot below. Choose a suitable scale for the line plot.

Height of Plants (feet)

Quiz 44: Using Line Plots to Solve Problems

1   Amber made the line plot below to record the height of each basil plant in her garden.

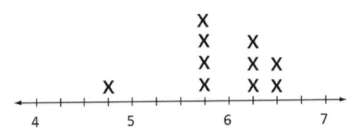

Height of Basil Plants (inches)

What is the difference in height between the tallest and the shortest basil plant?

Ⓐ 1 inch   Ⓑ $1\frac{3}{4}$ inches   Ⓒ $2\frac{1}{4}$ inches   Ⓓ 3 inches

2   Jeffrey recorded how far he ran each morning for five days. The distance he ran on the first four days is shown below.

X		X		X	X
$1\frac{3}{4}$	2	$2\frac{1}{4}$	$2\frac{1}{2}$	$2\frac{3}{4}$	3

Distance Ran (miles)

Jeffrey ran a total of 12 miles on the five days. How far did Jeffrey run on the fifth day?

Show your work.

Answer _____ miles

3 Enzo recorded the time he spent practicing the guitar each week. The time he spent practicing in weeks 1 and 2 is shown below. He practiced for a total time of 35 hours over three weeks. Complete the line plot by adding the time he spent practicing in week 3.

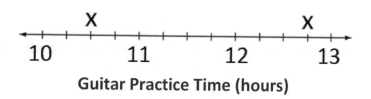

Guitar Practice Time (hours)

Write an expression below to show that he practiced for a total of 35 hours.

Expression

4 The line plot below shows the lengths of the stems of each rose plant in Chris's garden.

```
                 X
                 X          X
                 X          X          X
      X          X          X          X
   _____
      2         2¼         2½         2¾         3
```

Length of Rose Stems (feet)

What fraction of the rose plants have stems of 2 inches? _____

What fraction of the rose plants have stems of $2\frac{1}{2}$ inches? _____

What fraction of the rose plants have stems of $2\frac{1}{2}$ inches or more? _____

5   Abigail recorded the amount of snowfall at her home for the first seven days of December. She wrote this list of facts about the data she recorded.

- The snowfall each day was at least $1\frac{1}{2}$ inches.
- The snowfall each day was no more than 3 inches.
- The total snowfall was $15\frac{3}{4}$ inches.

If the snowfall was 2 inches on five of the days, what must it have been on the remaining two days? Complete the line plot below with the data for the seven days. Then write the answer below.

$1\frac{1}{2}$	$1\frac{3}{4}$	2	$2\frac{1}{4}$	$2\frac{1}{2}$	$2\frac{3}{4}$	3

Amount of Daily Snowfall (inches)

Answer _____ inches and _____ inches

Is it possible for the snowfall to have been the same each day for seven days and have a total of $15\frac{3}{4}$ inches? Explain your answer.

_____

_____

_____

6 Sandy recorded the mass of all the apples she picked from an apple tree. The line plot below shows the data.

```
                        X
                        X                   X
                        X       X           X                       X
            X       X   X       X           X                       X
            X       X   X       X           X           X           X
        _____
           3 1/8    3 1/4   3 3/8   3 1/2   3 5/8   3 3/4   3 7/8
```

Mass of Apples (ounces)

What is the difference in mass between the heaviest and the lightest apple?

Show your work.

Answer _____ ounces

What is the difference in mass between the least common mass and the most common mass?

Show your work.

Answer _____ ounces

Sandy wants to select three apples with a total mass of 10 ounces. List two different sets of apples she could select.

1. _____ ounces, _____ ounces, and _____ ounces

2. _____ ounces, _____ ounces, and _____ ounces

Quiz 45: Understanding Angles and Angle Measurement

1   What is the measure of the angle shown below?

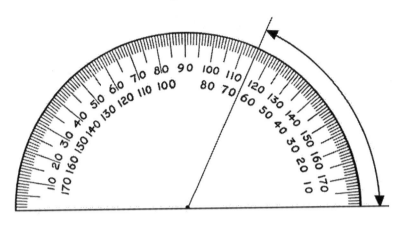

Ⓐ 65°   Ⓑ 75°   Ⓒ 115°   Ⓓ 125°

2   What is the measure of the angle shown below?

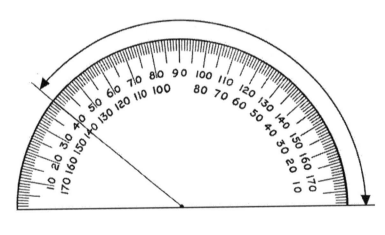

Ⓐ 40°   Ⓑ 50°   Ⓒ 140°   Ⓓ 180°

3   Which angle appears to be greater than 90°?

4   Tick the correct box to place each angle below in the correct category.

	Less than 90°	Between 90° and 180°	Greater than 180°
	☐	☐	☐
	☐	☐	☐
	☐	☐	☐
	☐	☐	☐
	☐	☐	☐
	☐	☐	☐

5   Draw an angle with the given measure in each circle below.

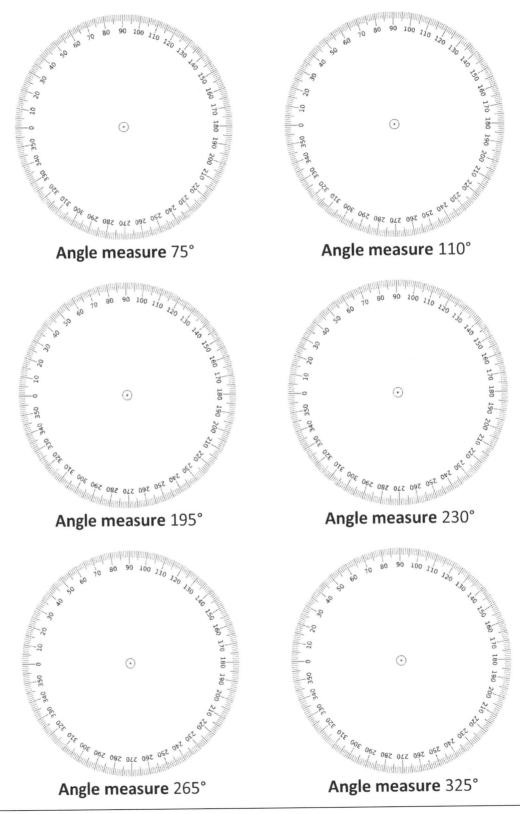

Angle measure 75°   **Angle measure** 110°

Angle measure 195°   **Angle measure** 230°

Angle measure 265°   **Angle measure** 325°

6   The diagram shows an angle of 266° and a missing angle labeled *x*.

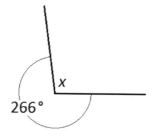

What is the measure of the angle marked *x*? Show or explain how you found your answer.

Answer _____°

7   Samuel divided a circle into five equal sections, as shown below.

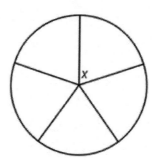

What is the measure of the angle marked *x*? Show or explain how you found your answer.

Answer _____°

Quiz 46: Measuring Angles

1   Find the measure of each angle shown below.

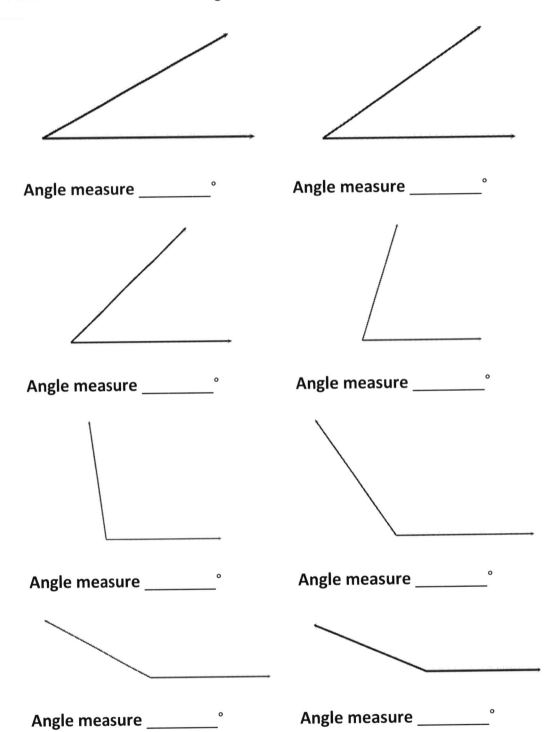

Angle measure _____°   Angle measure _____°

Angle measure _____°   Angle measure _____°

Angle measure _____°   Angle measure _____°

Angle measure _____°   Angle measure _____°

2   Find the three angle measures for each triangle shown below. List the angle measures below each triangle.

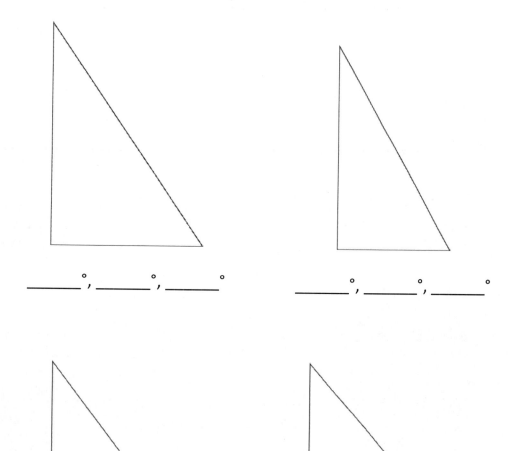

_____°, _____°, _____°   _____°, _____°, _____°

_____°, _____°, _____°   _____°, _____°, _____°

What do the four triangles have in common?

_____

_____

3   Each shape has two pairs of equal angles. Find the measures of each pair of angles. List the angle measures below each shape.

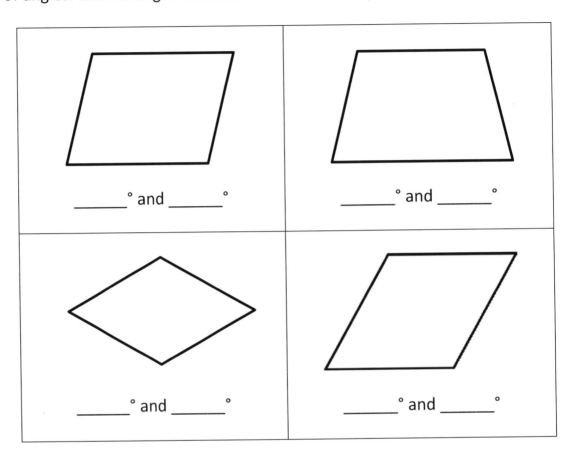

4   Find the measure of each angle of the hexagon below. Label the hexagon with the correct angle measures.

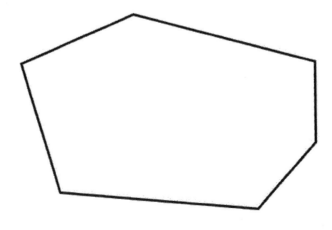

Quiz 47: Sketching Angles

1   Sketch an angle with the given measure in each space below.

Angle measure 25°	**Angle measure** 40°
Angle measure 82°	**Angle measure** 94°
Angle measure 105°	**Angle measure** 136°
Angle measure 152°	**Angle measure** 172°

2   One side of a triangle is shown below. Complete the triangle so that it has angles of 90°, 20°, and 70°.

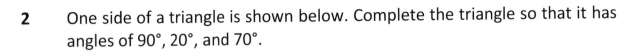

3   One side of a trapezoid is shown below. Complete the trapezoid so that it has two angles of 120° and two angles of 60°.

4   One side of a rhombus is shown below. Complete the rhombus so that it has two angles of 45° and two angles of 135°.

5 In the space below, draw a pentagon with 5 equal angles of 108°.

6 Rebecca sketched the two angles shown below.

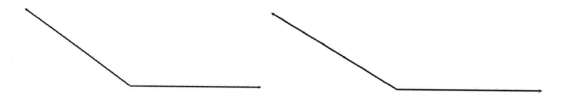

In the space below, sketch two different angles with a measure between the two angles Rebecca sketched. Label each angle with its angle measure.

7 Complete the second angle below to show an angle 20° more than the first angle. Label the angle with its angle measure.

Quiz 48: Decomposing Angles

1   If the angle below is divided into 3 equal parts, what will be the measure of each angle?

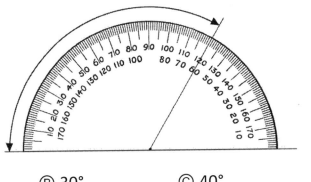

Ⓐ 20°   Ⓑ 30°   Ⓒ 40°   Ⓓ 60°

2   What is the measure of the unknown angle?

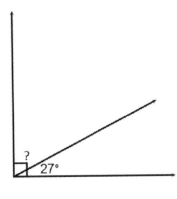

Ⓐ 54°   Ⓑ 63°   Ⓒ 73°   Ⓓ 81°

3   What is the measure of the unknown angle?

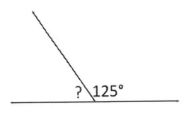

Ⓐ 25°   Ⓑ 55°   Ⓒ 75°   Ⓓ 115°

4 Complete the table with the missing angle measure.

Angles	Small Angle	Large Angle
	40°	
	78°	
		113°
		118°

5   Divide the angle shown below into two equal parts.

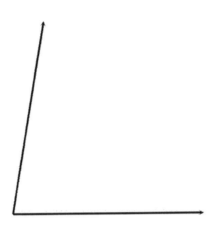

What is the measure of each angle? _____°

Complete the number sentence to show the sum of the angles.

_____° + _____° = _____°

6   Divide the angle shown below into four equal parts.

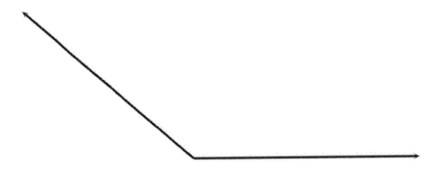

What is the measure of each angle? _____°

Complete the number sentence to show the sum of the angles.

_____° + _____° + _____° + _____° = _____°

7   Complete the expression that can be used to find the missing angle in the diagram below. Then solve the equation to find the answer.

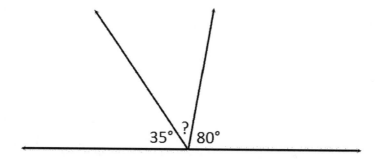

_____ - _____ - _____ = _____

Answer _____ °

8   Find the missing angle in the diagram below.

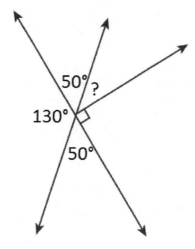

Show your work or explain how you found your answer.

Answer _____ °

Quiz 49: Solving Problems Involving Angles

1   How many one-degree angles can the angle below be divided into?

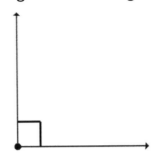

Ⓐ 45   Ⓑ 90   Ⓒ 180   Ⓓ 360

2   A pizza is divided into 8 equal pieces, as shown below.

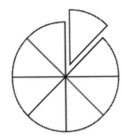

Which expression can be used to find the angle at the point of each piece?

Ⓐ 90 ÷ 8   Ⓑ 180 ÷ 8   Ⓒ 240 ÷ 8   Ⓓ 360 ÷ 8

3   The straight angle below is divided into four angles.

Three of the angles measure 32°, 44°, and 63°. What is the measure of the fourth angle?

Ⓐ 41°   Ⓑ 61°   Ⓒ 139°   Ⓓ 221°

4   Which two angles could be combined to form a right angle?

Ⓐ 55° and 45°   Ⓑ 62° and 18°   Ⓒ 31° and 59°   Ⓓ 22° and 38°

5   A list of angles is given below.

21°	165°	143°	13°	25°	44°
62°	11°	30°	28°	33°	37°
35°	127°	69°	138°	156°	9°

List two pairs of angles that can be combined to form a right angle.

_____° and _____° or _____° and _____°

List three angles that can be combined to form a right angle.

_____° and _____° and _____°

List two angles that can be combined to form a straight angle.

_____° and _____°

List three angles that can be combined to form a straight angle.

_____° and _____° and _____°

6   Complete the diagram below to show that the sum of 105°, 35°, and 40° is 180°.

7 A diagram is shown below.

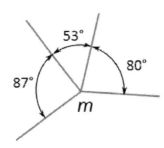

Write and solve an equation to find the measure of the missing angle.

Answer _____°

8 The triangle below has two angles of 72° and one angle of 36°. Draw a line on the triangle to divide it into two triangles with the same angle measures.

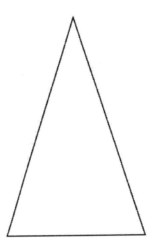

What are the angle measures of each new triangle?

Answer _____° and _____° and _____°

9 Ginger drew a right triangle. She labeled an exterior angle, as shown below.

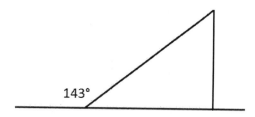

143°

If all the interior angles of the triangle add to 180°, what are the three angle measures? Show or explain how you found your answer.

Answer _____° and _____° and _____°

10 Latoya made a banner by cutting a triangle from the top of a rectangular piece of cardboard, as shown below.

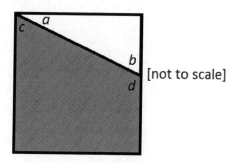

[not to scale]

The angle labeled *a* is 26° and the angle labeled *b* is 64°. What are the measures of the angles labeled *c* and *d*? Show or explain how you found your answer.

Answer *c* = _____°, *d* = _____°

Quiz 50: Finding the Area of Complex Shapes

1   Which of these finds the area of the shape below, in square units?

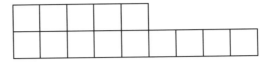

Ⓐ (2 × 2) + 4 = 8   Ⓑ (2 × 4) + 5 = 13

Ⓒ (5 × 2) + 4 = 14   Ⓓ (5 × 4) + 5 = 25

2   What is the area of the shaded figure on the grid, in square units?

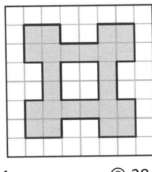

Ⓐ 20   Ⓑ 24   Ⓒ 28   Ⓓ 32

3   Allison made a shape by placing two pieces of cardboard together, as shown below.

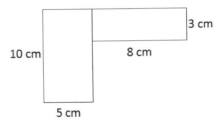

She adds a third piece of cardboard to make a shape with a total area of 130 square centimeters. Which of these could be the shape of the third piece of cardboard?

Ⓐ 5 cm by 10 cm   Ⓑ 3 cm by 13 cm

Ⓒ 8 cm by 7 cm   Ⓓ 6 cm by 9 cm

4   Complete the expressions to show how to find the area of each shape, in square units.

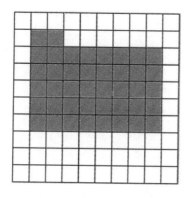

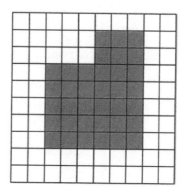

(___ × ___) + (___ × ___)   (___ × ___) + (___ × ___)

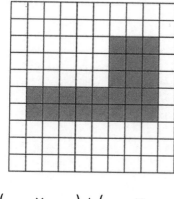

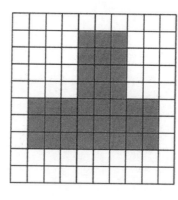

(___ × ___) + (___ × ___)   (___ × ___) + (___ × ___)

5   Draw a shape on each grid whose area can be found by the calculation shown.

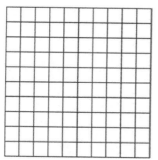

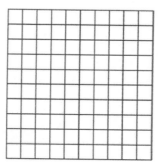

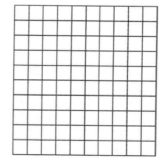

(6 × 2) + (4 × 3) = 24   (5 × 2) + (3 × 3) = 19   (8 × 1) + (2 × 4) = 16

6   Sally used the expression (5 × 4) + (8 × 2) to find the area of a kitchen bench, in square feet. On the grid below, draw one possible shape of the kitchen bench. Then find the area of the kitchen bench.

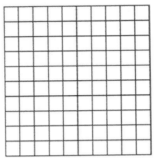

Answer _____ square feet

7   The diagram below shows the shape of George's kitchen floor.

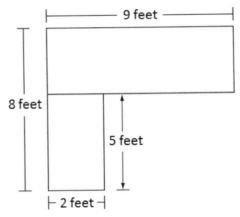

George wants to tile the kitchen floor with 1-foot square tiles. Each tile costs $3. What is the total cost of the tiles George needs?

Show your work.

Answer $_____

8 A model of the shape of a swimming pool is shown below. A fence is built around the pool 2 meters from each edge.

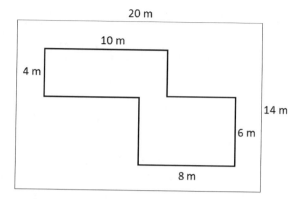

What is the area of the base of the swimming pool? Use words or equations to show how you found your answer.

Answer _____ square meters

The area around the pool inside the fence is tiled. What is the area of the tiled area? Use words or equations to show how you found your answer.

Answer _____ square meters

9 Kieran covered the top of a desk with wooden panels, as shown below.

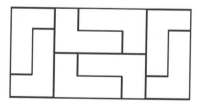

Each panel had an area of 4 square feet. What is the total area covered by the panels? Show or explain how you found your answer.

Answer _____ square feet

Quizzes 51 to 56

Geometry

Directions

Read each question carefully. For each multiple-choice question, fill in the circle for the correct answer. For other types of questions, follow the directions given in the question.

You may use a ruler and a protractor to help you answer questions. You should answer the questions without using a calculator.

MATHEMATICS SKILLS LIST
For Parents, Teachers, and Tutors

Quizzes 51 through 56 cover these skills from the Georgia Standards of Excellence.

Geometry

Draw and identify lines and angles, and classify shapes by properties of their lines and angles.

1. Draw points, lines, line segments, rays, angles (right, acute, obtuse), and perpendicular and parallel lines. Identify these in two-dimensional figures.

2. Classify two-dimensional figures based on the presence or absence of parallel or perpendicular lines, or the presence or absence of angles of a specified size. Recognize right triangles as a category, and identify right triangles.

3. Recognize a line of symmetry for a two-dimensional figure as a line across the figure such that the figure can be folded along the line into matching parts. Identify line-symmetric figures and draw lines of symmetry.

Quiz 51: Identifying and Drawing Points, Lines, Line Segments, and Rays

1   Which term best describes each side of the triangle below?

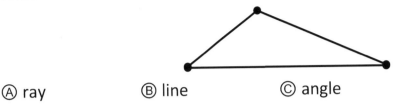

Ⓐ ray   Ⓑ line   Ⓒ angle   Ⓓ line segment

2   Which of these is shown below?

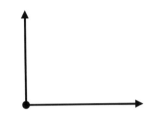

Ⓐ two rays forming an angle

Ⓑ two line segments forming an angle

Ⓒ two line segments forming a ray

Ⓓ two rays forming a line segment

3   Which two statements explain why the diagram below shows lines? Select the two correct answers.

☐ They are straight.

☐ They form angles.

☐ They have endpoints.

☐ They continue in both directions without ending.

☐ They meet and cross over each other.

4 Label the diagram below with the correct terms. Write the correct term below in each empty box.

ray   point   endpoint   line segment

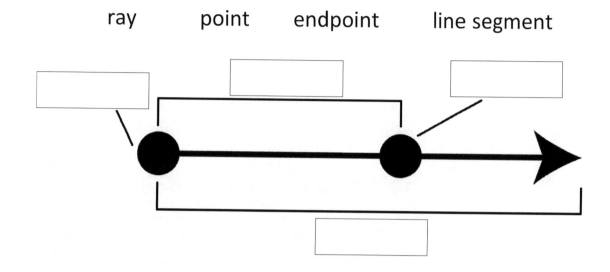

5 A ray is shown below.

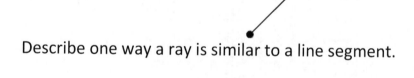

Describe one way a ray is similar to a line segment.

_____

_____

Describe one way a ray is different from a line segment.

_____

_____

Describe one way a ray is different from a line.

_____

_____

6   The points *A* and *B* are shown on the grid below. Draw the square *ABCD* by plotting the points *C* and *D* and connecting the four points.

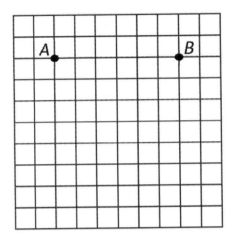

7   Draw two points 8 units apart on the grid below. Label the points *Y* and *Z* and connect the two points.

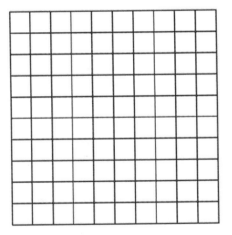

Circle the term that describes *YZ*.

ray   line   line segment   angle

Explain why you circled the term you chose.

_____

_____

8   The grid below has points *A*, *B*, and *C* plotted. Draw the following items on the grid.

- A line segment that connects points *A* and *B*
- A line that passes through points *B* and *C*
- A ray with an endpoint at point *C* that extends to the left
- A ray with an endpoint at point *A* that extends downwards

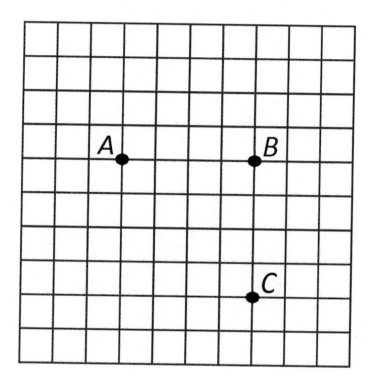

9   Draw endpoints or arrows on the end of each diagram below to show the difference between a line, a ray, and a line segment.

Line   _____

Ray   _____

Line segment   _____

Quiz 52: Identifying and Drawing Angles

1   Which shape below appears to have only obtuse angles?

2   Which term describes angle *P*?

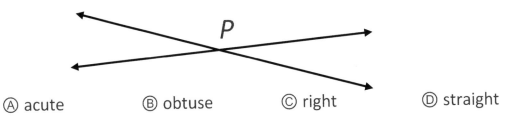

Ⓐ acute   Ⓑ obtuse   Ⓒ right   Ⓓ straight

3   The top of a gift box is in the shape of a star, as shown below.

How many acute angles does the star have? _____ acute angles

4   Select all the shapes that have exactly two acute angles.

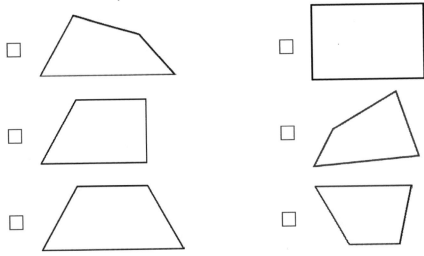

5   For each shape shown below, circle all the acute angles.

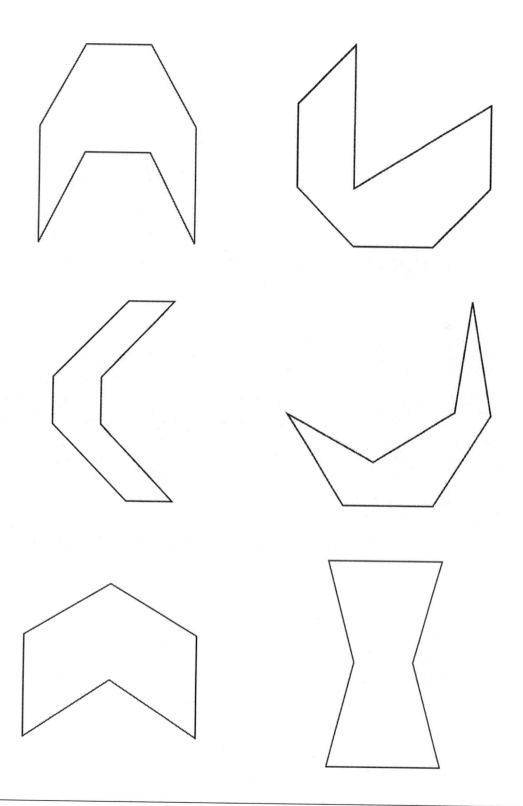

6 Complete the drawing of an acute angle below. Then write the symbol <, >, or = in the empty box to explain why the angle is acute.

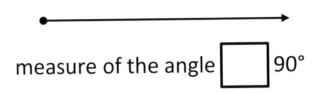

measure of the angle ☐ 90°

Complete the drawing of an obtuse angle below. Then write the symbol <, >, or = in each empty box to explain why the angle is obtuse.

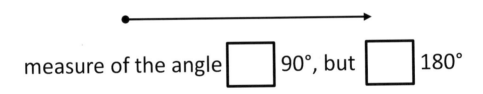

measure of the angle ☐ 90°, but ☐ 180°

Complete the drawing of a right angle below. Then write the symbol <, >, or = in the empty box to explain why the angle is right.

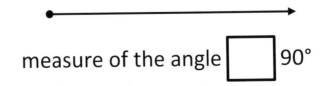

measure of the angle ☐ 90°

7   On each grid below, draw a shape with the description given.

Draw a triangle with one obtuse angle.	
Draw a triangle with three acute angles.	
Draw a quadrilateral with two obtuse angles and two acute angles.	
Draw a quadrilateral with two right angles, one acute angle, and one obtuse angle.	

Quiz 53: Identifying and Drawing Perpendicular and Parallel Lines

1   Which of these represents a perpendicular relationship in the diagram below?

Ⓐ the relationship between the bottom of the ladder and the ground

Ⓑ the relationship between the top of the ladder and the ground

Ⓒ the relationship between the tree and the ladder

Ⓓ the relationship between the tree and the ground

2   Which of these are shown in the diagram below?

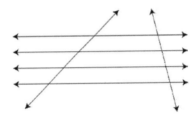

Ⓐ only parallel lines

Ⓑ only perpendicular lines

Ⓒ both parallel and perpendicular lines

Ⓓ neither parallel nor perpendicular lines

3   Which shape has two pairs of parallel sides?

4 Draw a second line below that is perpendicular to the line shown.

What is the measure of the angle between the two lines? _____°

5 Draw a second line below that intersects the line shown but is not perpendicular to it.

Describe the types of angles that are formed.

_____

_____

6 Divide triangle *ABC* into two shapes by drawing a line segment parallel to line segment *AB*. Divide triangle *XYZ* into two shapes by drawing a line segment parallel to line segment *YZ*.

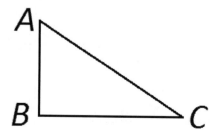 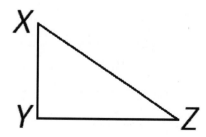

7 Three lines are shown below.

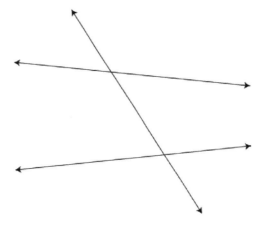

Are any of the lines parallel to each other? Explain how you can tell.

_____

_____

Are any of the lines perpendicular to each other? Explain how you can tell.

_____

_____

8 Abby states that the two pairs of lines below are both parallel because they do not intersect.

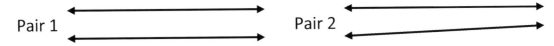

Pair 1   Pair 2

Explain why Abby is incorrect.

_____

_____

_____

9   A diagonal is a line that goes from one corner of a shape to the opposite corner. Draw the two diagonals on each shape below.

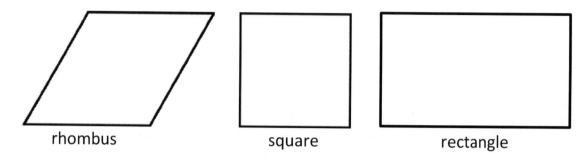

rhombus   square   rectangle

Which shape or shapes have perpendicular diagonals? Explain how you found your answer.

_____

_____

_____

10   The line segments below are labeled with the letters P, Q, R, S, and T.

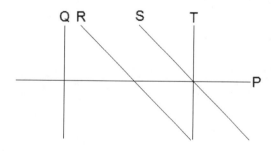

Which two pairs of line segments are parallel?

_____ and _____, _____ and _____

Which two pairs of line segments are perpendicular?

_____ and _____, _____ and _____

Quiz 54: Classifying Two-Dimensional Figures

1 Jamal wants to determine whether a triangle is obtuse. Which question would Jamal be best to answer?

Ⓐ Does the triangle have any sides of equal length?

Ⓑ Does the triangle have an angle greater than a right angle?

Ⓒ Does the triangle have a line of symmetry?

Ⓓ Does the triangle have any equal angles?

2 A triangle has a pair of perpendicular sides. Which statement must be a correct description of the triangle?

Ⓐ It is a right triangle.

Ⓑ It is a scalene triangle.

Ⓒ It is an equilateral triangle.

Ⓓ It is an equiangular triangle.

3 Which triangle shown below is a scalene triangle?

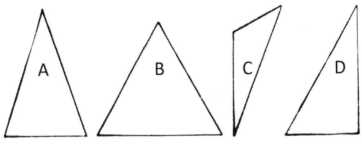

Ⓐ triangle A   Ⓑ triangle B   Ⓒ triangle C   Ⓓ triangle D

4 Circle all the triangles below that are obtuse triangles.

5   Carter drew a shape with at least one right angle. Select all the shapes that Carter could have drawn.

     ☑ square   ☐ trapezoid   ☐ equilateral triangle

     ☑ rectangle   ☐ obtuse triangle   ☑ right triangle

6   Tiffany drew a shape with exactly one right angle. Select all the shapes that Tiffany could have drawn.

     ☐ square   ☐ trapezoid   ☐ rhombus

     ☐ rectangle   ☐ obtuse triangle   ☑ right triangle

7   The shapes below have been sorted into two groups.

Group A   **Group B**

Explain what property was used to sort the shapes.

They used quaderaliters to figure it out.

8 Select all the properties below that are always true of each shape. Tick each box to show a property that is always true of the shape.

	at least one right angle	at least one pair of perpendicular sides	at least one pair of parallel sides	two pairs of perpendicular sides
right triangle	☑	☒	☑	☒
rectangle	☑	☑	☑	☑
trapezoid	☑	☒	☑	☒
square	☑	☑	☑	☑

9 Sort the shapes below based on the categories in the table. Write the letters of the shapes that fit the category in each column. Each shape may fit into more than one category and some shapes may not fit in any.

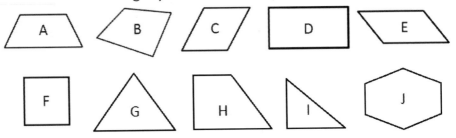

Shapes with at Least One Right Angle	Shapes with at Least One Pair of Perpendicular Sides	Shapes with at Least One Pair of Parallel Sides
F H I D	G J	A C D F E

10   On each grid below, draw a shape with the features listed. Then name the shape.

- two obtuse angles
- two acute angles
- two pairs of parallel sides

Name _____

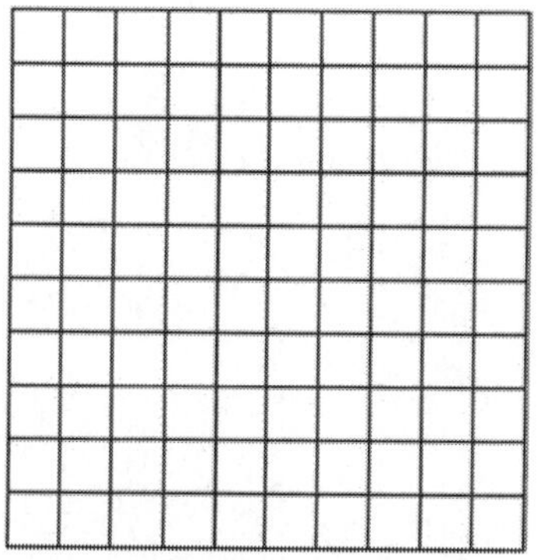

- one pair of perpendicular sides
- no parallel sides
- three sides in all

Name _____

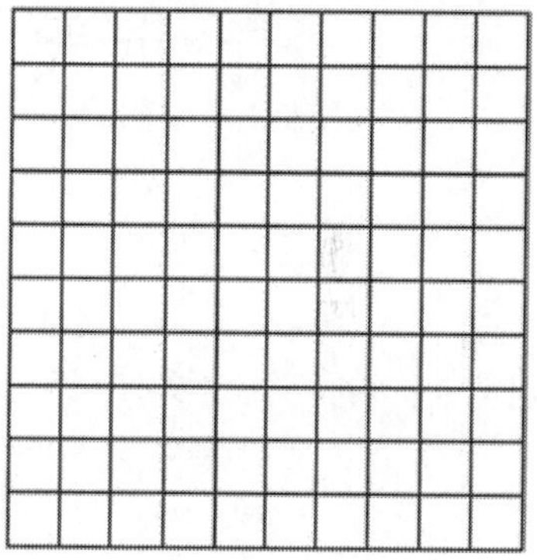

11   Draw a triangle below with 3 equal sides.

Are the angles also equal? Explain your answer.

_____

_____

_____

Quiz 55: Understanding Symmetry

1 Which figure below has a line of symmetry?

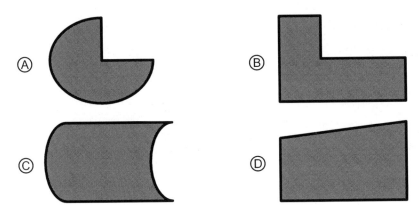

2 Which diagram shows a line of symmetry?

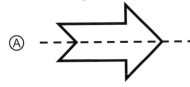

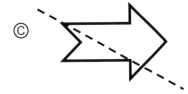
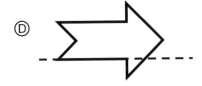

3 Circle all the shapes below that have at least one line of symmetry.

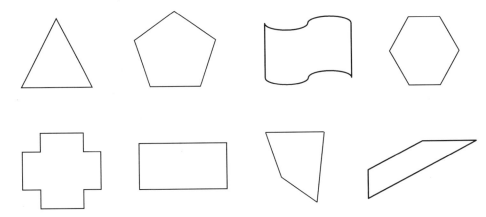

4 The diagrams below show one half of a figure and the line of symmetry of the figure. Complete each diagram by drawing the whole figure.

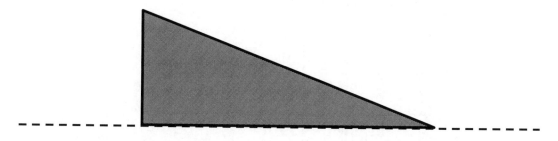

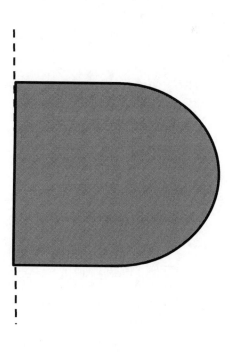

5   The grids below show half of a figure and a line of symmetry. Shade squares on the grid to show the complete figure.

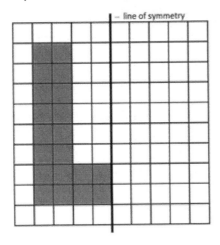

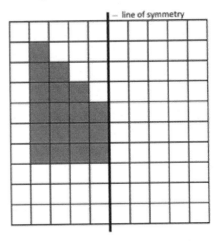

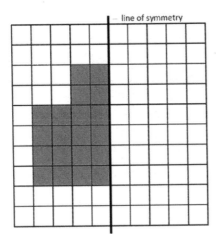

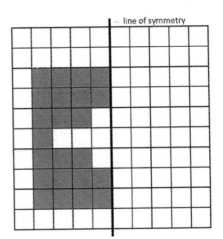

6   The grids below show quarter of a figure and two lines of symmetry. Shade squares on the grid to show the complete figure.

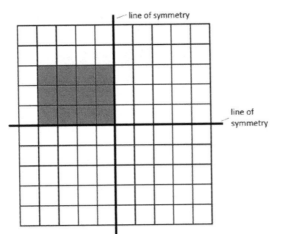

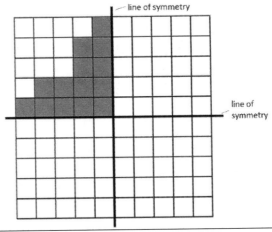

7   Liam used blocks to make the pattern shown below.

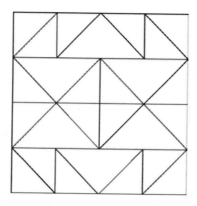

Does the block pattern have symmetry? Explain how you can tell.

_____

_____

_____

8   Bianca cuts out the shape shown below. Draw a line to show where Bianca should fold the shape to show that it has a line of symmetry.

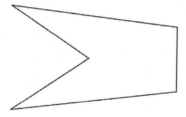

Describe how Bianca could tell whether the shape has a line of symmetry by folding it along the line.

_____

_____

_____

Quiz 56: Identifying and Drawing Lines of Symmetry

1 Which letter below has a line of symmetry?

Ⓐ F   Ⓑ G   Ⓒ L   Ⓓ W

2 Which letter below has more than one line of symmetry?

Ⓐ H   Ⓑ K   Ⓒ S   Ⓓ U

3 Which diagram shows a line of symmetry?

Ⓐ 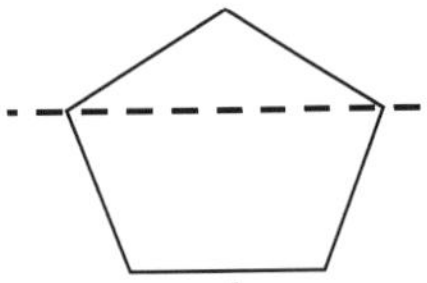   Ⓑ

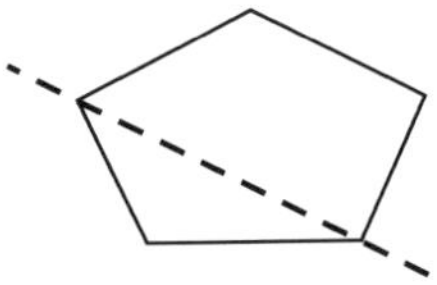

Ⓒ 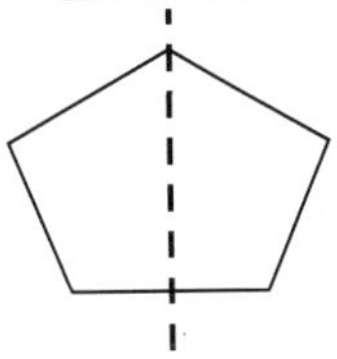   Ⓓ

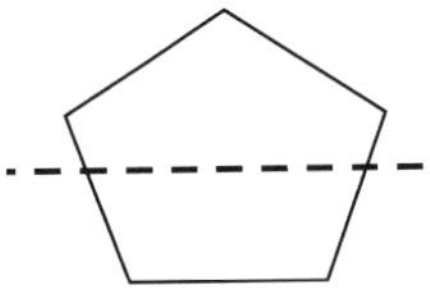

4 Which figure appears to have exactly one line of symmetry?

Ⓐ 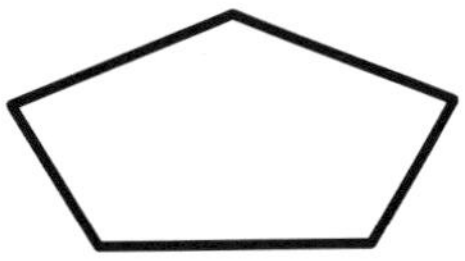   Ⓑ

Ⓒ   Ⓓ

5 How many lines of symmetry does the shape below have?

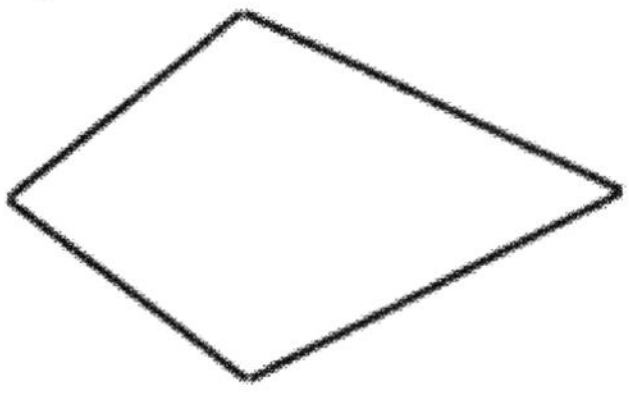

Answer _____

6 Draw all the lines of symmetry on the figure below.

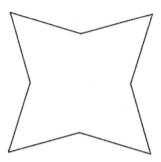

7 Draw a line of symmetry on each letter shown below.

A C D

E M T

V X Y

8   Look at the figures below.

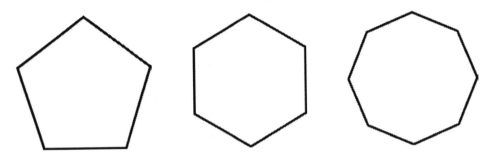

Which figure has the most lines of symmetry? Explain how you found your answer.

_____

_____

_____

9   Jade states that the dotted line is a line of symmetry because the shape on each side has the same area.

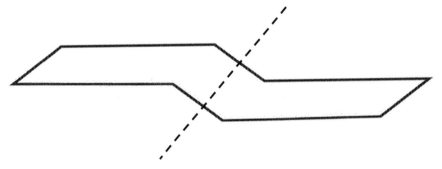

Explain whether or not Jade is correct.

_____

_____

_____

10 Percy drew the four quadrilaterals shown below.

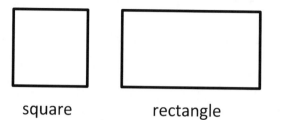 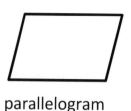

square   rectangle   trapezoid   parallelogram

Which shape he drew does not have a line of symmetry? _____

How many lines of symmetry does the square have? ____

How many lines of symmetry does the rectangle have? ____

How many lines of symmetry does the trapezoid have? ____

11 Four triangles labeled A, B, C, and D are shown below.

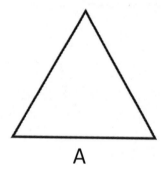  

A   B   C   D

Which triangle has exactly one line of symmetry? ____

Which triangle has three lines of symmetry? ____

Which two triangles do not have a line of symmetry? ____ and ____

Explain how you can tell that the two triangles are not symmetrical.

_____

_____

_____

ANSWER KEY

Quizzes 1 to 13: Operations and Algebraic Thinking

Quiz 1: Understanding Multiplication

1. C **2.** A **3.** D **4.** C **5.** 2, 7, 14 = 2 × 7; 3, 7, 21 = 3 × 7; 5, 7, 35 = 5 × 7; 7, 7, 49 = 7 × 7; 11, 5, 55 = 11 × 5 **6.** 3, 9, 15, 3, 5, 42 miles **7.** addition, 14 + 3, 17 years old; multiplication, 5 × 3, $15; multiplication, 6 × 5, 30 floors; addition, 80 + 15, 95 students; multiplication, 18 × 4, 72 cameras **8.** 4 notebooks; The student may describe counting by 3s to reach 12, or explain that 4 lots of 3 equals 12. **9.** number line shows 15, 30, 45, 60, 75; 75 minutes **10.** number line shows 20, 40, 60, 80; $80

Quiz 2: Using Multiplication Equations

1. A **2.** D **3.** B **4.** B **5.** 2nd, 3rd, 4th **6.** 1st, 5th **7.** 6 × 8 = 48, 48 stickers; 9 × 4 = 36, 36 apples; 12 × 8 = 96, $96; 5 × 15 = 75, $75; 60 × 3 = 180, 180 miles **8.** 4 × 7 = 28, 28 baseball cards; 6 × 3 = 18, 18 aces; 15 × 4 = 60, 60 minutes; 12 × 5 = 60, $60; 4 × 6 = 24, 24 pens **9.** 4 × n = 24, 6 cookies; 4 × c = 12, $3 **10.** 6 × b = 72 or 72 ÷ 6 = b; 12 boxes **11.** 4 × g = 8; 2 years old **12.** 12 × 4 = m; 48 muffins **13.** 3 × 4 = p, 3 × 6 = p; 12 pts, 18 pts, 33 pts

Quiz 3: Using Multiplication to Solve Problems

1. B **2.** C **3.** D **4.** D **5.** 2nd, 7th **6.** 4, 2, 3, 1 **7.** 8, 200, $2; 28, 700, $7; 20, 500, $5; 12, 300, $3 **8.** $432 (18 × 8 = 144, 144 × 3 = 432) **9.** $240 (12 × 16 = 192, 8 × 6 = 48, 192 + 48 = 240) **10.** 6 quarters, 18 dimes, 72 nickels, 60 pennies (6 × 3 = 18 dimes, 18 × 4 = 72 nickels, 6 × 10 = 60 pennies) **11.** 72 points (18 × 3 = 54, 54 + 18 = 72); 42 points (7 × 6 = 42) **12.** $160 (January $16, February $16 × 3 = $48, March $48 × 2 = $96, $16 + $48 + $96 = $160) **13.** 32 pieces (8 × 4 = 32); 192 pieces (8 × 2 = 16 pieces long, 4 × 3 = 12 pieces wide, 16 × 12 = 192)

Quiz 4: Using Division to Solve Problems

1. B **2.** A **3.** 4 books **4.** 1st, 4th, 6th **5.** 84 ÷ 3, 28; 84 ÷ 4, 21; 84 ÷ 6, 14; 84 ÷ 7, 12 **6.** 70 ÷ 5 = 14, 14 dimes; 24 ÷ 8 = 3, $3; 108 ÷ 9 = 12, 12 cars; 48 ÷ 8 = 6, 6 bags; 96 ÷ 3 = 32, 32 students **7.** 48 ÷ 4 = 12, 12 years old; 80 ÷ 5 = 16, 16 minutes; 45 ÷ 5 = 9, $9; 85 ÷ 5 = 17, $17; 78 ÷ 6 = 13, 13 pieces **8.** 12 triangles for Monday, 9 triangles for Tuesday **9.** 15 boxes (360 ÷ 24 = 15 or 24 × ? = 360) **10.** 480 loaves (360 plain loaves, 360 ÷ 3 = 120 multigrain loaves, 360 + 120 = 480); 18 loaves (1,386 ÷ 3 = 462 loaves sold, 480 − 462 = 18) **11.** number line shows 12, 24, 36, 48; 4 rafts

Quiz 5: Understanding Remainders

1. A **2.** A **3.** B **4.** B **5.** 10 r 2, 8 r 5, 10 r 2, 13 r 1, 8 r 3, 4 r 2, 5 r 3, 6 r 7, 9 r 5, 5 r 8 **6.** 12, 2; 10, 8; 9, 8; 8, 10; 8, 2; There will be 11 heats with 8 runners, and 1 heat with 10 runners. **7.** 3 sets of 8 apples circled, 6 apples left over; 3 groups; 6 apples **8.** diagram of 4 rows of 6 lettuces with 4 lettuces left over; $28 \div 6 = 4$ r 4 **9.** number line shows 12, 24, 36, 48; 4 vases filled, 2 flowers left over **10.** The student should explain that 63 cannot be evenly divided by 6, or that $63 \div 6 = 10$ r 3.; 3 shelves of 21, 21 shelves of 3, 7 shelves of 9, or 9 shelves of 7 **11.** Each of the 8 groups will get 40 flashcards each, and there will be 18 flashcards left over. **12.** There will be 7 tables of 6 people, and there will be 4 people left over.

Quiz 6: Solving Multi-step Problems

1. C **2.** C **3.** B **4.** A **5.** Wed, Thurs, Fri **6.** 135 seconds ($4 \times 30 = 120$, $120 + 15 = 135$) **7.** 36 plates ($24 \times 6 = 144$ pieces, $144 \div 4 = 36$ plates) **8.** $792 ($24 \times \$8 = \$192$ for trucks, $24 \times 5 = 120$ cars, $\$5 \times 120 = \$600$ for cars, $\$192 + \$600 = \$792$ total) **9.** 4 weeks ($45 + 15 + 15 + 15 + 15 = 105$ or $100 - 45 = 55$ and $55 \div 15 = 3$ r 10) **10.** 257 seconds ($65 + 68 + 73 + 69 = 275$, $275 - 18 = 257$) **11.** Dyno $385, Royal $305, Hawk $525, Jetson $625 ($85 \times 4 + 45 = 385$, $65 \times 4 + 45 = 305$, $120 \times 4 + 45 = 525$, $145 \times 4 + 45 = 625$) **12.** $7,680 ($4 \times 160 = 640$ total tickets, $12 \times 640 = 7,680$); $1,806 ($38 \times 7 = 266$, $110 \times 12 = 1,320$, $22 \times 10 = 220$, $266 + 1,320 + 220 = 1,806$; $3,432 ($12 \times 7 = 84$, $75 \times 12 = 900$, $16 \times 10 = 160$, $84 + 900 + 160 = 1,144$, $1,144 \times 3 = 3,432$)

Quiz 7: Representing Word Problems with Equations

1. C **2.** D **3.** D **4.** 1st, 2nd, 4th, 5th **5.** $n \times 12 = 72$, 6; $n - 25 = 68$, 93; $88 \div n = 4$, 22; $n + 54 = 89$, 35; $n \div 3 = 27$, 81; $n \times 7 = 140$, 20; $n = 9 \times 14$, 126 **6.** $30 \div 6 = s$; $8 \times 6 = t$; $(3 \times 6) + c = 20$ **7.** $25 + 10 \times 4 = c$ **8.** $(4 \times 5) \times d = 300$, 15 days **9.** $17 + 19 + m = 60$, 24 minutes **10.** $(2 \times 6) + (4 \times 4) + (2 \times n) = 40$, 6 notebooks **11.** $3 + (3 \times 2) = r$, 9 rainy days **12.** $(18 \times 9) + (22 \times 14) = d$, $470; $(24 + 35) - (15 + 12) = s$, 32 pizzas; $(c \times 9) + (30 \times 14) = 600$, 20 pizzas

Quiz 8: Using Estimation and Rounding

1. C **2.** B **3.** A **4.** C **5.** Ann and Leah, Toby, Leah **6.** C **7.** D **8.** A **9.** $80 \times 6 = 480$, $90 \times 6 = 540$, between 480 and 540; $40 \times 5 = 200$, $50 \times 5 = 250$, between 200 and 250; $90 \times 7 = 630$, $100 \times 7 = 700$, between 630 and 700; $70 \times 9 = 630$, $80 \times 9 = 720$, between 630 and 720; $30 \times 8 = 240$, $40 \times 8 = 320$, between 240 and 320 **10.** $25 \div 5 = 5$, $30 \div 5 = 6$, between 5 and 6; $32 \div 4 = 8$, $36 \div 4 = 9$, between 8 and 9; $36 \div 6 = 6$, $42 \div 6 = 7$, between 6 and 7; $80 \div 8 = 10$, $88 \div 8 = 11$, between 10 and 11 **11.** 3 messages ($90 \div 30 = 3$ or $96 \div 31 = 3$) **12.** 400 books ($50 \times 8 = 400$) **13.** 4,000 cans ($20 \times 200 = 4000$); The estimate is less than the actual amount ordered. Both numbers are rounded down, so the estimate is lower. **14.** Parker has rounded down the number of hats to find the estimate. He will have enough to buy 60 hats for $5 each, but not enough to buy 67 hats. **15.** Molly will have saved just under $280. $7 \times 40 = 280$ and 38 is less than 40, so 7×38 will be less than 280.

Quiz 9: Understanding and Using Factors

1. D **2.** D **3.** A **4.** D **5.** 2, 3, 6 **6.** 2, 4, 19 **7.** 14 × 2, 7 × 4; 22 × 2, 11 × 4; 25 × 2, 5 × 10; 21 × 3, 7 × 9; 33 × 2, 22 × 3, 11 × 6; 39 × 2, 26 × 3, 13 × 6; 44 × 2, 22 × 4, 8 × 11 **8.** 5 or 11; 5 or 13; 6 or 8 or 12; 6 or 7 or 14; 7 or 8 or 14; 6 or 8 or 9 or 12 **9.** 1, 2, 4, 7, 14, and 28; 1, 5, 7, and 35; 1, 2, 5, 7, 10, 14, 35, and 70; 1 and 7 **10.** 75 ÷ 3 = 25, 3 and 25; 96 ÷ 6 = 16, 6 and 16; 76 ÷ 4 = 19, 4 and 19; 98 ÷ 14 = 7, 14 and 7; 84 ÷ 21 = 4, 21 and 4 **11.** A factor pair of 39 is 13 and 3.
12. number line shows 15, 30, 45, 60, 75, 90; 6 and 15; number line is divided to show any of the following factor pairs with the factor pair listed: 2 and 45, 3 and 30, 5 and 18, or 9 and 10.
13. 3, 15, 9, 5; The student should explain that the length and width of each rectangle shows two numbers that multiply to give 45, or that the length and width of each rectangle show two numbers that can be divided evenly into 45.

Quiz 10: Understanding and Using Multiples

1. C **2.** C **3.** D **4.** A **5.** 24, 48, 60, 84 **6.** 5, 10, 15, 20, 30, 60 **7.** 10, 20, 30, 40, 50, 60, 70, 80, 90, 100; 11, 22, 33, 44, 55, 66, 77, 88, 99; 12, 24, 36, 48, 60, 72, 84, 96; 14, 28, 42, 56, 70, 84, 98; 15, 30, 45, 60, 75, 90; 18, 36, 54, 72, 90; 20, 40, 60, 80, 100 **8.** 4, 8, 12, 16, 20, 24, 28, 32, 36, 40, 44, 48; 6, 12, 18, 24, 30, 36, 42, 48; 8, 16, 24, 32, 40, 48; 12, 24, 36, 48; 24, 48 **9.** 13, 26, 39, 52, 65, 78, 91, 104; The first 8 multiples of 13 are 13, 26, 39, 52, 65, 78, 91, and 104.
10. rectangle drawn 17 squares long and 5 squares high; 17, 34, 51, 68, 85 **11.** 16, 32, and 48
12. number line shows 9, 18, 27, 36, 45; 9, 18, 27, 36, and 45 **13.** 24, 36, and 48 circled; The student should explain that the other numbers are not multiples of 6.

Quiz 11: Identifying Prime and Composite Numbers

1. D **2.** C **3.** B **4.** C **5.** D **6.** 31, 37, 53, 59 **7.** Joya and Mona; The student should explain that 5 and 7 cannot be divided evenly by any numbers other than themselves and 1, and so are prime numbers. The numbers 8 and 9 can be evenly divided by other numbers, and so are composite numbers. **8.** The student should explain that all the numbers can be evenly divided by 5. **9.** The student should explain that Lauren is correct because all the even numbers greater than 2 can be evenly divided by 2, and so must be composite numbers.

Quiz 12: Generating Patterns

1. D **2.** B **3.** C **4.** C **5.** 64, 72, 96 **6.** 5, 9, 13, 17, 21, 25; 80, 77, 74, 71, 68, 65; 2, 4, 8, 16, 32, 64; 5, 12, 19, 26, 33, 40; 35, 29, 23, 17, 11, 5; 16, 25, 34, 43, 52, 61; 1, 3, 9, 27, 81, 243; 10, 18, 26, 34, 42, 50; 3, 6, 12, 24, 48, 96; 4, 40, 400, 4000, 40000, 400000 **7.** 280, 264, 248, 232, 216, 200, 184 **8.** 2, 8; 3, 12; 4, 16; 5, 20; 6, 24 **9.** 6, 18; 9, 27; 14, 42; 17, 51; 21, 63; 26, 78 **10.** Term 4 is drawn to show 16 squares; 2, 2 **11.** Set 4 is drawn to show 3 marbles, Set 5 is drawn to show 1 marble; Each set in the pattern has 2 less marbles than the one before it. **12.** The student should explain that 185 will be a number because it is a multiple of 5.

Quiz 13: Describing and Analyzing Patterns

1. C **2.** D **3.** C **4.** A **5.** $10 \times 12 = 120$, $13 \times 12 = 156$, table completed with 120 and 156; $192 \div 12 = 16$, $216 \div 12 = 18$, table completed with 16 and 18 **6.** 2, 4, 6, 8, 10, 12, 14, 16, rule is "Add 2" or "$n + 2$"; 2, 4, 8, 16, 32, 64, 128, 256, rule is "Multiply by 2" or "$n \times 2$" **7.** 20, 23, $n + 3$; 96, 192, $n \times 2$; 20, 16, $n - 4$; 31, 36, $n + 5$; 45, 34, $n - 11$; 1024, 4096, $n \times 4$ **8.** 8, 20, 32, 44, 56, 68; 75, 69, 63, 57, 51, 45; The student should explain that the first pattern is always adding an even number to an even number, and that the second pattern is always subtracting an even number from an odd number. **9.** 192, 96, 48, 24, 12, 6, 3 **10.** 94, 86, 78, 70, 62, 54, 46, 38, 30, 22, 14, 6; 12 rounds; 6 dancers; 72, 80, and 88 are circled; The student should explain that only multiples of 8 or numbers that can be evenly divided by 8 will have 8 dancers left in the final round.

Quizzes 14 to 23: Number and Operations in Base Ten

Quiz 14: Understanding Place Value

1. C **2.** B **3.** C **4.** B **5.** D **6.** C **7.** 3rd, 4th, 6th **8.** 2nd, 6th **9.** 85, 850, 8,500, 85,000; 751, 7,510, 75,100, 751,000; 642, 6,420, 64,200, 642,000; 95, 950, 9,500, 95,000; 346, 3,460, 34,600, 346,000; 2,058, 20,580, 205,800, 2,058,000; 673, 6,730, 67,300, 673,000 **10.** 10, 10, 100, 1,000, 100, 10, 10, 100, 10,000 **11.** 10, $80 \times 10 = 800$; 100, $7 \times 100 = 700$; 100, $35 \times 100 = 3,500$; 1,000, $26 \times 1,000 = 26,000$; 100, $380 \times 100 = 38,000$ **12.** 2,500 pennies ($25 \times 100 = 2,500$) **13.** 14,000 nails ($14 \times 1,000 = 14,000$) **14.** $100 ($2,800 \div 28 = 100$) **15.** The student should explain that the 6 in 600,000 is 10 times greater than the 6 in 60,000.

Quiz 15: Reading and Writing Whole Numbers

1. D **2.** D **3.** 200 **4.** 136 **5.** 2nd, 3rd, 4th **6.** A **7.** 20,005; 20,050; 20,500; 25,000; 800,900; 890,000; 800,009; 809,000; 800,090 **8.** 4, 3, 5; 7, 2, 9; 6, 8, 0; 2, 5, 1, 7; 6, 3, 5, 9; 3, 6, 5, 9; 2, 8, 7, 3; 4, 5, 6, 2 **9.** 5,726; 36,859; 69,035; 410,307; 276,030; 908,524; 1,000,467; 7,509,006 **10.** 8, 5, 7, 2, 3; 8, 5, 7, 23; 85, 7, 2, 3; 85, 72, 3 **11.** 9,000; 900; 500; 50; 400; 4; 9,000, 900, 500, 50, 400, 4

Quiz 16: Comparing Whole Numbers

1. C **2.** B **3.** B **4.** A **5.** 1st, 3rd, 4th **6.** 2, 3, 4, 1 **7.** 4,675; 25,909; 608,549; 1,284; 76,159; 2,555,425; 554,227; 877,929; 262,487; 165,335 **8.** 3,586; 8,653; 3,856; 3,685; 3,685; 5,836 **9.** drawing of 1 block of 10 and 7 blocks of 1; 10; 100 **10.** >, >, =, >, <, >, = **11.** 8; 8, 7; The student should explain that 80 and 87 have the same number of tens, but 87 has more ones. **12.** 2, 9, 7; 2, 7, 7; The student should explain that 277 has fewer tens than 297. **13.** 26,349 < 26,408 < 28,688 < 28,715 < 28,968; any four numbers between 28,688 and 28,968

Quiz 17: Rounding Whole Numbers

1. A **2.** C **3.** D **4.** 863, 857 **5.** 530, 509, 481, 524 **6.** 600,000; 580,000; 583,730; 583,700 **7.** 6,400 / 6,000; 5,200 / 5,000; 2,000 / 2,000; 3,300 / 3,000; 64,800 / 65,000; 35,700 / 36,000; 18,100 / 18,000; 25,800 / 26,000; 168,300 / 168,000; 357,900 / 358,000 **8.** 550 / 649; 4,150 / 4,249; 68,450 / 68,549; 128,750 / 128,849; 8,745,250 / 8,745,349 **9.** hundred, thousand, ten, thousand, hundred **10.** Thursday; Wednesday; Tuesday; Friday; Wednesday and Thursday **11.** 36, 67, 15, 206, 365, 6,087, 3,426 are circled; The student should explain that all the numbers that are rounded up have a digit 5 or greater in the ones place. **12.** 190,000; 185,000; The student should describe using the digit in the thousands place to round to the nearest ten thousand, and using the digit in the hundreds place to round to the nearest thousand. **13.** The student may describe how Gary did not consider that the number could be less than 2,000, or may explain that the numbers from 1,500 to 1,999 are also rounded to 2,000.

Quiz 18: Adding Whole Numbers

1. D **2.** C **3.** D **4.** D **5.** D **6.** B **7.** 1st, 2nd **8.** 8,943 + 2,593 **9.** 20, 40, 400, 31, 319, 50, 500, 12, 4,000, 6,000, 6,000, 300, 1,900, 10,000, 23,000 **10.** 577, 951, 882, 1,020, 919, 1,742, 960, 2,852, 8,579, 4,231, 13,694, 16,110, 4,692, 11,782, 6,929, 7,489, 60,578, 53,470, 37,429, 113,758, 500,900, 952,357, 237,010, 888,040 **11.** 20 + 90 = 110, 9 + 7 = 16, 110 + 16 = 126; 40 + 70 = 110, 1 + 8 = 9, 110 + 9 = 119; 80 + 80 = 160, 6 + 5 = 11, 160 + 11 = 171; 70 + 10 = 80, 5 + 9 = 14, 80 + 14 = 94 **12.** 688,000 (300,000 + 100,000 + 200,000 = 600,000; 40,000 + 30,000 + 10,000 = 80,000; 2,000 + 2,000 + 4,000 = 8,000; 600,000 + 80,000 + 8,000 = 688,000) **13.** 4,301,261 (2,165,983 + 2,135,278 = 4,301,261)

Quiz 19: Subtracting Whole Numbers

1. C **2.** A **3.** A **4.** C **5.** A **6.** 3rd, 4th, 5th **7.** 5th **8.** 60, 30, 5, 500, 40, 400, 20, 6, 405, 420, 2,000, 80, 400, 9,000, 2,100 **9.** 4,892,320; 4,896,020; 4,846,320; 4,296,320; 2,896,320; 4,896,300 **10.** 492, 97, 199, 144, 111, 233, 148, 281, 5,955, 3,380, 5,149, 3,348, 157,550, 508,626, 307, 610,546 **11.** $22,288 (27,874 + 25,655 = 53,529; 16,904 + 14,337 = 31,241; 53,529 - 31,241 = 22,288 or 27,874 + 25,655 - 16,904 - 14,337 = 22,288) **12.** 749,920 people (3,325,210 – 2,575,290 = 749,920); 1,154,165 people (1,330,961 – 176,796 = 1,154,165); 578,134 people (754,930 – 176,796 = 578,134)

Quiz 20: Multiplying Whole Numbers

1. B **2.** D **3.** C **4.** 1st, 2nd, 5th **5.** 225, 315, 630, 1,350, 2,025, 2,700 **6.** 63, 84, 66, 3,000, 32, 120, 360, 1,400, 36, 99, 66, 3,200 **7.** 185, 408, 116, 360, 795, 768, 4,536, 1,785, 25,455, 61,072, 6,027, 51,906, 3,195, 338, 1,632, 7,176

Quiz 21: Understanding and Representing Multiplication

1. C **2.** D **3.** C **4.** 108, 168, 324 **5.** 23 × 6 = 138 **6.** 4th, 5th **7.** 1,161 (model has 800, 280, 60, 21); 5,248 (model has 4,800, 320, 120, 8); 3,325 (model has 2,700, 150, 450, 25); 4,484 (model has 3,500, 630, 300, 54) **8.** (60 × 9) + (8 × 9) = 540 + 72 = 612; (30 × 6) + (7 × 6) = 180 + 42 = 222; (70 × 8) + (2 × 8) = 560 + 16 = 576; (90 × 5) + (4 × 5) = 450 + 20 = 470; (50 × 7) + (3 × 7) = 350 + 21 = 371; (80 × 4) + (5 × 4) = 320 + 20 = 340 **9.** 14 × 29 = 406, $406 **10.** 7 × 659 = 4,613, $4,613 **11.** 576 square inches (The student may count the tiles or use the equation 4 × 3 = 12. The student should calculate 12 × 48 = 576.) **12.** a 16 by 7 rectangle is shaded; 112; The student should explain that you can count the shaded squares.

Quiz 22: Dividing Whole Numbers

1. A **2.** B **3.** A **4.** C **5.** 1,400 square meters **6.** 3rd, 6th **7.** 3rd, 5th **8.** 32, 441, 2,124, 500, 33, 132, 2,122, 1,100, 21, 110, 1,001, 1,302 **9.** 71, 295, 192, 155, 86, 83, 1,354, 653, 706

Quiz 23: Understanding and Representing Division

1. C **2.** C **3.** A **4.** C **5.** 2nd, 3rd, 4th, 5th **6.** $4 \times 98 = 392$; $5 \times 173 = 865$; $6 \times 87 = 522$; $8 \times 116 = 928$; $7 \times 254 = 1,778$; $9 \times 430 = 3,870$ **7.** Eva, 31 squares ($155 \div 5 = 31$); Hayley, 17 squares ($153 \div 9 = 17$); Wade and Sanjay, 9 squares ($112 \div 8 = 14$, $184 \div 8 = 23$, $23 - 14 = 9$) **8.** $38 \div 7 = 5$ r 3; There are 38 cans sorted into groups of 7 cans each. There are 5 groups of 7 and 3 cans left over. **9.** 7 groups of 8 coins are circled with 4 uncircled coins left over; 7 days; 4 quarters **10.** $140 \div 4 = 35$, $900 \div 3 = 300$ **11.** 642 tickets ($3,852 \div 6 = 642$); 344 tickets ($2,408 \div 7 = 344$); 749 adults ($3,852 + 642 = 4,494$; $4,494 \div 6 = 749$)

Quizzes 24 to 36: Number and Operations – Fractions

Quiz 24: Understanding Equivalent Fractions

1. C **2.** C **3.** $\frac{2}{6}, \frac{4}{12}, \frac{1}{3}$ **4.** $\frac{16}{20} = \frac{8}{10} = \frac{4}{5}$ **5.** 2 of 4 parts shaded, $\frac{2}{4}$; 3 of 6 parts shaded, $\frac{3}{6}$; 4 of 8 parts shaded, $\frac{4}{8}$; 6 of 12 parts shaded, $\frac{6}{12}$ **6.** 2 of 5 parts shaded; 4 of 10 parts shaded, $\frac{4}{10}$ **7.** 4 of 12 parts shaded; 2 of 6 parts shaded, $\frac{2}{6}$; 1 of 3 parts shaded, $\frac{1}{3}$ **8.** $\frac{1}{5}$ or $\frac{4}{20}$; $\frac{1}{5}$ or $\frac{2}{10}$; $\frac{4}{20} = \frac{2}{10}$ **9.** fractions $\frac{2}{3}, \frac{4}{6}$, and $\frac{8}{12}$ plotted; $\frac{4}{6}$ and $\frac{8}{12}$ **10.** fractions $\frac{4}{5}$ and $\frac{8}{10}$ plotted; $\frac{8}{10}$; The student should explain that the two fractions are at the same point on the number line. **11.** rectangle with 5 of 6 equal parts shaded and rectangle with 10 of 12 equal parts shaded; The student should explain that the two fractions have the same area of the rectangle shaded.

Quiz 25: Identifying and Generating Equivalent Fractions

1. A **2.** D **3.** A **4.** C **5.** B **6.** 4th, 5th, 7th, 8th **7.** $\frac{6}{8}, \frac{9}{12}, \frac{15}{20}$ **8.** 3 of 10 parts shaded, $\frac{30}{100}, \frac{3}{10}$; 4 of 5 parts shaded, $\frac{80}{100}, \frac{4}{5}$; 1 of 4 parts shaded, $\frac{25}{100}, \frac{1}{4}$ **9.** fractions $\frac{1}{3}, \frac{2}{6}$, and $\frac{4}{12}$ plotted; The student should explain that the three fractions are at the same points on the number line. **10.** $\frac{6}{12}, \frac{4}{6}$, and $\frac{75}{100}$ circled; $\frac{1}{2}, \frac{2}{3}, \frac{3}{4}$; The student should explain that the numerator and denominator cannot be divided evenly by any number. **11.** Ben has 8 ticks and 4 crosses, Drake has 2 ticks and 1 cross; Ben $\frac{8}{12}$ scored, $\frac{4}{12}$ missed; Drake $\frac{2}{3}$ scored, $\frac{1}{3}$ missed **12.** 4 questions (The student should show or explain that $\frac{80}{100}$ is equivalent to $\frac{4}{5}$.)

Quiz 26: Comparing Fractions

1. D **2.** A **3.** D **4.** 2, 1, 3, 4 **5.** $\frac{5}{6}, \frac{1}{2}, \frac{3}{4}, \frac{1}{3}$ **6.** $\frac{2}{3} = \frac{8}{12}; \frac{1}{2} = \frac{6}{12}; \frac{3}{4} = \frac{9}{12}; \frac{5}{6} = \frac{10}{12}; \frac{5}{12}, \frac{1}{2}, \frac{7}{12}, \frac{2}{3}, \frac{3}{4}, \frac{5}{6}$ **7.** $\frac{3}{5}, \frac{7}{10}, \frac{4}{5}, \frac{21}{25}, \frac{85}{100}, \frac{9}{10}$ (The work should show all the fractions being converted to fractions with denominators of 100 so they can be compared.) **8.** =, 2 parts shaded, 2 parts shaded; >, 6 parts shaded, 5 parts shaded; <, 1 part shaded, 2 parts shaded; <, 4 parts shaded, 7 parts shaded **9.** Audrey (The work should show all the fractions being converted to fractions with denominators of 12 so they can be compared.) **10.** $\frac{9}{10}, \frac{3}{4}$, and $\frac{7}{12}$ are circled; The student should explain that fractions greater than $\frac{1}{2}$ have a numerator more than half the denominator.; $\frac{5}{10}$; The student should explain that fractions equal to $\frac{1}{2}$ have a numerator exactly half the denominator. **11.** 5 of 6 equal parts shaded; 7 of 12 equal parts shaded; The student should explain that $\frac{5}{6} > \frac{7}{12}$ because more of the rectangle is shaded, or that $\frac{7}{12} < \frac{5}{6}$ because less of the rectangle is shaded.

Quiz 27: Understanding Addition and Subtraction of Fractions

1. A **2.** D **3.** B **4.** A **5.** $\frac{3}{10}$ **6.** $\frac{4}{6} + \frac{1}{6} = \frac{5}{6}$; $\frac{6}{12} + \frac{3}{12} = \frac{9}{12}$; $\frac{8}{10} + \frac{1}{10} = \frac{9}{10}$; $\frac{11}{12} - \frac{9}{12} = \frac{2}{12}$; $\frac{7}{8} - \frac{4}{8} = \frac{3}{8}$; $\frac{4}{12} + \frac{4}{12} + \frac{3}{12} = \frac{11}{12}$; $\frac{60}{100} + \frac{30}{100} + \frac{7}{100} = \frac{97}{100}$; $\frac{9}{12} - \frac{2}{12} - \frac{5}{12} = \frac{2}{12}$ **7.** 2 of 3 parts shaded, $\frac{2}{3}$; 3 of 5 parts shaded, $\frac{3}{5}$; 4 of 6 parts shaded, $\frac{4}{6}$ or $\frac{2}{3}$; 6 of 12 parts shaded, $\frac{6}{12}$ or $\frac{1}{2}$ **8.** 2 of 4 parts shaded, $\frac{2}{4}$ or $\frac{1}{2}$; 2 of 8 parts shaded, $\frac{2}{8}$ or $\frac{1}{4}$; 3 of 12 parts shaded, $\frac{3}{12}$ or $\frac{1}{4}$ **9.** 7 of 8 parts shaded, $\frac{7}{8}$ inches **10.** number line has points at $\frac{1}{2}, \frac{3}{4}$, and $1\frac{1}{2}$, $1\frac{1}{2}$ hours **11.** $\frac{7}{8}$ ounces ($\frac{5}{8} + \frac{3}{4} = \frac{5}{8} + \frac{6}{8} = \frac{11}{8}$; $\frac{11}{8} - \frac{1}{2} = \frac{11}{8} - \frac{4}{8} = \frac{7}{8}$)

Quiz 28: Decomposing Fractions

1. D **2.** C **3.** B **4.** 4th, 5th **5.** $\frac{2}{6}, \frac{6}{12}, \frac{1}{8}, \frac{7}{10}, \frac{2}{3}, \frac{2}{5}$ **6.** $\frac{3}{6}, \frac{1}{5}, \frac{4}{10}, \frac{4}{8}, \frac{6}{12}, \frac{11}{100}$ **7.** 2 of 8 parts shaded, 1 of 4 parts shaded, $\frac{1}{8} + \frac{1}{8} = \frac{1}{4}$; 4 of 10 parts shaded, 2 of 5 parts shaded, $\frac{1}{10} + \frac{1}{10} + \frac{1}{10} + \frac{1}{10} = \frac{2}{5}$ **8.** 5 of 8 parts shaded, $\frac{5}{8}$ **9.** 2 of 4 parts shaded, 2 of 4 parts shaded, 4 of 4 parts shaded, $\frac{2}{4} + \frac{2}{4} = 1$; 1 of 4 parts shaded, 3 of 4 parts shaded, 4 of 4 parts shaded, $\frac{1}{4} + \frac{3}{4} = 1$ **10.** 2 of 6 parts shaded, 2 of 6 parts shaded, 2 of 6 parts shaded, 6 of 6 parts shaded, $\frac{2}{6} + \frac{2}{6} + \frac{2}{6} = 1$; 1 of 6 parts shaded, 2 of 6 parts shaded, 3 of 6 parts shaded, 6 of 6 parts shaded, $\frac{1}{6} + \frac{2}{6} + \frac{3}{6} = 1$ **11.** $\frac{4}{10}$ or $\frac{2}{5}$ (6 of the 10 parts are shaded, 4 of the 10 parts remain) **12.** rectangle divided into 8 equal parts and 7 of the 8 parts shaded, $\frac{1}{8}$ of the money saved

Quiz 29: Adding and Subtracting Mixed Numbers

1. C **2.** B **3.** C **4.** B **5.** 5th, 6th, 7th **6.** $\frac{11}{4} + \frac{27}{4}, \frac{38}{4}, 9\frac{1}{2}$; $\frac{11}{6} + \frac{14}{6}, \frac{25}{6}, 4\frac{1}{6}$; $\frac{27}{8} + \frac{28}{8}, \frac{55}{8}, 6\frac{7}{8}$; $\frac{47}{10} + \frac{16}{10}, \frac{63}{10}, 6\frac{3}{10}$; $\frac{178}{100} + \frac{135}{100}, \frac{313}{100}, 3\frac{13}{100}$; $\frac{33}{4} - \frac{26}{4}, \frac{7}{4}, 1\frac{3}{4}$; $\frac{37}{6} - \frac{20}{6}, \frac{17}{6}, 2\frac{5}{6}$; $\frac{42}{8} - \frac{23}{8}, \frac{19}{8}, 2\frac{3}{8}$; $\frac{34}{10} - \frac{15}{10}, \frac{19}{10}, 1\frac{9}{10}$; $\frac{51}{12} - \frac{20}{12}, \frac{31}{12}, 2\frac{7}{12}$ **7.** 9 of 12 parts shaded + 6 of 8 parts shaded = 15 of 16 parts shaded; $3\frac{3}{4}$ **8.** 17 of 20 parts shaded + 19 of 20 parts shaded = 36 of 40 parts shaded; $3\frac{6}{10}$ or $3\frac{3}{5}$ **9.** number line shows points at $1\frac{1}{3}$, 3, and $4\frac{2}{3}$; $4\frac{2}{3}$ **10.** $8\frac{3}{12}$ or $8\frac{1}{4}$ ($\frac{43}{12} + \frac{56}{12} = \frac{99}{12} = 8\frac{3}{12}$ or $3 + 4 + \frac{7}{12} + \frac{8}{12} = 7 + \frac{15}{12} = 7 + 1\frac{3}{12} = 8\frac{3}{12}$) **11.** $7\frac{4}{5}$ ($\frac{14}{5} + \frac{7}{5} + \frac{18}{5} = \frac{39}{5} = 7\frac{4}{5}$ or $2 + 1 + 3 + \frac{4}{5} + \frac{2}{5} + \frac{3}{5} = 6 + \frac{9}{5} = 6 + 1\frac{4}{5} = 7\frac{4}{5}$) **12.** $3\frac{5}{6}$ ($\frac{39}{6} - \frac{16}{6} = \frac{23}{6} = 3\frac{5}{6}$) **13.** $1\frac{7}{8}$ ($\frac{43}{8} - \frac{10}{8} - \frac{18}{8} = \frac{15}{8} = 1\frac{7}{8}$)

Quiz 30: Solving Word Problems Involving Fractions

1. A **2.** C **3.** D **4.** 1st, 4th, 5th **5.** $4 - 2\frac{1}{8} = f$; $1\frac{7}{8}$ **6.** $2\frac{1}{6} + 1\frac{4}{6} = f$; $3\frac{5}{6}$ **7.** $3\frac{4}{8} + 4\frac{3}{8} = 7\frac{7}{8}$; $7\frac{7}{8}$ pounds
8. $5\frac{1}{12} - 4\frac{7}{12} = \frac{6}{12}$; $\frac{6}{12}$ feet or $\frac{1}{2}$ feet **9.** $3\frac{1}{5}$ miles ($4\frac{3}{5} - 1\frac{2}{5} = 3\frac{1}{5}$); $1\frac{4}{5}$ miles ($4\frac{3}{5} - 2\frac{4}{5} = 1\frac{4}{5}$); $1\frac{4}{5}$ miles
($3\frac{1}{5} - 1\frac{2}{5} = 1\frac{4}{5}$) **10.** $\frac{6}{8}$ or $\frac{3}{4}$ pizzas ($2\frac{7}{8} - 2\frac{1}{8} = \frac{6}{8}$); $7\frac{3}{8}$ pizzas ($2\frac{7}{8} + 2\frac{3}{8} + 2\frac{1}{8} = 7\frac{3}{8}$); $1\frac{5}{8}$ pizzas ($9 - 7\frac{3}{8} =$
$1\frac{5}{8}$ or $3 - 2\frac{7}{8} = \frac{1}{8}$, $3 - 2\frac{3}{8} = \frac{5}{8}$, $3 - 2\frac{1}{8} = \frac{7}{8}$, $\frac{1}{8} + \frac{5}{8} + \frac{7}{8} = 1\frac{5}{8}$)

Quiz 31: Understanding Fractions and Multiplication

1. C **2.** C **3.** B **4.** A **5.** 5, 7, 9, 11, 8, 4, 12, 31 **6.** $\frac{1}{2} + \frac{1}{2} + \frac{1}{2} + \frac{1}{2}$, 2; $\frac{2}{3} + \frac{2}{3} + \frac{2}{3}$, 2; $\frac{2}{5} + \frac{2}{5} + \frac{2}{5} + \frac{2}{5}$, $\frac{8}{5}$ or
$1\frac{3}{5}$; $\frac{5}{6} + \frac{5}{6} + \frac{5}{6}$, $\frac{15}{6}$ or $2\frac{3}{6}$ or $2\frac{1}{2}$; $\frac{3}{4} + \frac{3}{4} + \frac{3}{4} + \frac{3}{4} + \frac{3}{4}$, $\frac{15}{4}$ or $3\frac{3}{4}$; $\frac{7}{8} + \frac{7}{8} + \frac{7}{8} + \frac{7}{8}$, $\frac{28}{8}$ or $3\frac{4}{8}$ or $3\frac{1}{2}$ **7.** $5 \times \frac{1}{3}$; $\frac{5}{3}$
or $1\frac{2}{3}$ **8.** $8 \times \frac{1}{6}$; $\frac{8}{6}$ or $1\frac{2}{6}$ or $1\frac{1}{3}$ **9.** one part of each circle shaded; $\frac{6}{5}$ or $1\frac{1}{5}$ **10.** one part of each
circle shaded; $\frac{4}{8}$ or $\frac{1}{2}$ **11.** $\frac{1}{10} \times 9 = \frac{9}{10}$ **12.** 1 of 5 parts shaded × 4 = 4 of 5 parts shaded; $\frac{4}{5}$ **13.** 1 of
6 parts shaded × 7 = 7 of 12 parts shaded; $\frac{7}{6}$ or $1\frac{1}{6}$

Quiz 32: Multiplying Fractions by Whole Numbers

1. C **2.** A **3.** 3rd, 4th, 6th, 7th **4.** 1 of 4 parts of each shaded = 4 of 4 parts shaded; 1 of 2 parts of
each shaded = 2 of 2 parts shaded **5.** C **6.** 4, 8, 4, 3, 15, 18, 2, 40 **7.** $\frac{16}{10}$, $1\frac{6}{10}$ or $1\frac{3}{5}$; $\frac{18}{5}$, $3\frac{3}{5}$; $\frac{14}{6}$, $2\frac{2}{6}$
or $2\frac{1}{3}$; $\frac{15}{12}$, $1\frac{3}{12}$ or $1\frac{1}{4}$; $\frac{56}{8}$, 7; $\frac{20}{3}$, $6\frac{2}{3}$ **8.** $\frac{3}{4} \times 3$; $\frac{9}{4}$ or $2\frac{1}{4}$ **9.** $\frac{5}{6} \times 5$; $\frac{25}{6}$ or $4\frac{1}{6}$ **10.** 3 of 5 parts of each circle
shaded; $\frac{18}{5}$ or $3\frac{3}{5}$ **11.** 3 of 8 parts of each circle shaded; $\frac{15}{8}$ or $1\frac{7}{8}$ **12.** 2 of 5 parts shaded × 4 =
8 of 10 parts shaded; $\frac{8}{5}$ or $1\frac{3}{5}$ **13.** 5 of 6 parts shaded × 7 = 35 of 36 parts shaded; $\frac{35}{6}$ or $5\frac{5}{6}$

Quiz 33: Solving Word Problems Involving Multiplying Fractions

1. B **2.** B **3.** 6, 12, 18, 24 **4.** B **5.** 8 of 10 parts shaded; $\frac{4}{5}$ **6.** 5 parts shaded × 5 = 25 of 30 parts
shaded; $4\frac{1}{6}$ hours; The student should explain that the shaded answer represents $\frac{25}{6}$, which
equals $4\frac{1}{6}$ or that shading 25 squares completes 4 and $\frac{1}{6}$ squares. **7.** $10\frac{1}{12}$ inches ($\frac{11}{12} \times 11 = \frac{121}{12} =$
$10\frac{1}{12}$) **8.** Allison, Carmen, Li, Rebekah (Rebekah $\frac{3}{4}$ x 15 = $\frac{45}{4}$ = $11\frac{1}{4}$; Carmen $\frac{5}{6}$ x 10 = $\frac{50}{6}$ = $8\frac{1}{3}$;
Allison $\frac{2}{3}$ x 12 = $\frac{24}{3}$ = 8; Li $\frac{1}{2}$ x 18 = $\frac{18}{2}$ = 9) **9.** $6\frac{3}{4}$ liters ($\frac{3}{4}$ x 9 = $\frac{27}{4}$ = $6\frac{3}{4}$) **10.** 3 times (The student
may use the equation $\frac{1}{2} \times 3 = 1\frac{1}{2}$. The student may also use a diagram or a written
explanation.); 6 times (The student may use the equation $\frac{1}{4} \times 6 = 1\frac{1}{2}$. The student may also use
a diagram or a written explanation.)

Quiz 34: Understanding and Using Equivalent Decimal Fractions

1. A **2.** A **3.** 2nd, 4th **4.** B **5.** C **6.** $\frac{30}{100}, \frac{60}{100}, \frac{80}{100}, \frac{90}{100}$ **7.** $\frac{6}{10}; \frac{78}{100}; \frac{7}{10}$ and $\frac{69}{100}$ **8.** $\frac{60}{100} + \frac{31}{100} = \frac{91}{100}, \frac{10}{100} + \frac{29}{100} = \frac{39}{100}, \frac{40}{100} + \frac{7}{100} = \frac{47}{100}, \frac{80}{100} + \frac{11}{100} = \frac{91}{100}, \frac{20}{100} + \frac{57}{100} = \frac{77}{100}$ **9.** 7 of 10 parts shaded, $\frac{70}{100}$ and $\frac{7}{10}$; 4 of 10 parts shaded, $\frac{40}{100}$ and $\frac{4}{10}$ **10.** 57 of 100 parts shaded, $\frac{57}{100}$ **11.** $\frac{67}{100}$ (The student may shade an additional 20 squares to find a total amount shaded of 67 squares. The student may also calculate $\frac{47}{100} + \frac{20}{100} = \frac{67}{100}$.); $\frac{33}{100}$ (The student may use the diagram to show there are 33 unshaded squares. The student may also calculate $1 - \frac{67}{100} = \frac{33}{100}$.) **12.** The student should explain that Phoebe did not convert the fractions to fractions with the same denominators before adding them.; $\frac{80}{100} + \frac{9}{100} = \frac{89}{100}$.)

Quiz 35: Expressing Fractions as Decimals

1. C **2.** C **3.** D **4.** B **5.** A **6.** 3rd, 7th **7.** 0.31 **8.** 1.4 **9.** 9.6, 7.3 **10.** $\frac{5}{10}$, 0.5; $\frac{2}{10}$, 0.2; $4\frac{6}{10}$, 4.6; $6\frac{8}{10}$, 6.8 **11.** $\frac{45}{100}$, 0.45; $\frac{75}{100}$, 0.75; $\frac{92}{100}$, 0.92; $\frac{22}{100}$, 0.22; $5\frac{65}{100}$, 5.65 **12.** fractions $\frac{3}{10}, \frac{9}{10}, 1\frac{1}{10}$, and $1\frac{7}{10}$ plotted; 0.3, 0.9, 1.1, 1.7 **13.** 0.4, 0.8, 1.2, and 1.6 plotted; $\frac{2}{5}, \frac{4}{5}, 1\frac{1}{5}, 1\frac{3}{5}$ **14.** 13.73 seconds, 13.6 seconds

Quiz 36: Comparing Decimals

1. C **2.** B **3.** B **4.** 45.97, 45.82, 47.12, 47.55 **5.** 15 of 100 parts shaded, 2 of 10 parts shaded, 0.15 < 0.2; 4 of 100 parts shaded, 4 of 10 parts shaded, 0.04 < 0.4; 62 of 100 parts shaded, 6 of 10 parts shaded, 0.62 > 0.6; 80 of 100 parts shaded, 8 of 10 parts shaded, 0.80 = 0.8 **6.** 3 parts shaded, 8 parts shaded, 1 part shaded, 5 parts shaded; 0.1 < 0.3 < 0.5 < 0.8 **7.** <, =, <, >, <, > **8.** 3.09 cm; 3.62 cm; 3.59, 3.60, or 3.61 cm **9.** 0.2, 0.27, 0.14, 0.38, and 0.33 plotted; <, >, > **10.** 0.7, 1.1, and 1.6 plotted; 0.8, 0.9, and 1.0; 1.7, 1.8, and 1.9 **11.** The student may explain that Calie did not consider the place values of the digits, could state that the 5 is in the hundredths place while the 4 is in the tenths place, or may describe how Calie should have compared the digits 0 and 4 in the tenths place.

Quizzes 37 to 50: Measurement and Data

Quiz 37: Comparing Units

1. C **2.** B **3.** A **4.** A **5.** C **6.** 3, 4, 2, 1 **7.** kg, g, kg, g, g, g, kg **8.** 1st, 4th **9.** grain of rice, peanut, bean, French fry; apple, banana, egg, loaf of bread; pumpkin, watermelon, pineapple, turkey **10.** 30 cm, 305 mm, 34 cm, 3 m, 330 cm (The work should show converting all the measures to the same units to compare them.) **11.** 3 quarts; 1 pint; The student should explain that each glass will have about half a quart, which is equal to a pint. **12.** Kara (The work should show converting 1 minute to 60 seconds or converting 70 seconds to 1 minute and 10 seconds.)

Quiz 38: Converting Units of Measurement

1. B **2.** C **3.** A **4.** C **5.** 5th, 6th, 8th **6.** B **7.** 48 inches, 5 feet, 2 yards, 7 feet, 88 inches (The work should show converting all the measures to the same units to compare.) **8.** 1, 4, 8; 2, 8, 16; 4, 16, 32; 8, 32, 64; 10, 40, 80 **9.** 60 yards or 2,160 inches (180 ÷ 3 = 60, 180 × 12 = 2,160) **10.** 2 quarts (1 quart = 2 pints, 2 quarts = 4 pints) **11.** 190 minutes (3 × 60 + 10 = 170) **12.** 6,280 grams (6 kilograms = 6,000 grams; 6,000 + 280 = 6,280) **13.** 165 millimeters (24 cm = 240 mm; 240 − 75 = 165) **14.** 2,060 feet (5,280 × 2 = 10,560; 10,560 − 8,500 = 2,060)

Quiz 39: Solving Measurement Word Problems

1. C **2.** B **3.** C **4.** 500 grams **5.** 5 liters (20 × $\frac{1}{4}$ = 5) **6.** 16 glasses (24 quarts = 48 pints, 48 ÷ 3 = 16) **7.** 4$\frac{1}{4}$ liters (2$\frac{3}{4}$ + 1$\frac{1}{2}$ = 4$\frac{1}{4}$) **8.** 50 minutes (2:25 to 5:45 is 3 hours and 20 minutes or 200 minutes; 200 ÷ 4 = 50) **9.** 20 cups (500 + 750 + 750 = 2,000 mL; 2,000 ÷ 100 = 20) **10.** 154 inches (2$\frac{1}{2}$ feet = 30 inches, length of path is 30 + 1 + 30 + 1 + 30 + 1 + 30 + 1 + 30 = 154); 20 inches ($\frac{1}{2}$ foot = 6 inches, width of path is 6 + 1 + 6 + 1 + 6 = 20) **11.** $5 (It costs 5 × 4 = 20 quarters to do 4 loads of washing, and 20 × $\frac{1}{4}$ = 5.)

Quiz 40: Representing Measurement Problems

1. A **2.** D **3.** 30 × 3 = f or f ÷ 3 = 30, 90 feet; 3 × y = 18 or 18 ÷ 3 = y, 6 yards **4.** 6 of 36 parts shaded, 6 inches; 12 of 36 parts shaded, 12 inches **5.** 16 of 16 parts shaded, 16 of 16 parts shaded, and 4 of 16 parts shaded; 36 ounces **6.** 10 of 10 parts shaded, 10 of 10 parts shaded, 2 of 10 parts shaded; 2.2 centimeters **7.** 59 plotted for Anna, 61.5 plotted for Corey, 58 plotted for Morgan; Corey is 61.5 inches tall. Morgan is 58 inches tall. **8.** $6.50 (number line shows adding 0.5 to 3 seven times) **9.** 1:15 and 3:45 plotted; 2 hours, 30 minutes **10.** 6:15, 7:00, 7:45, 8:30, 9:15, and 10:00 plotted; 15 minutes; 20 minutes **11.** 2$\frac{1}{3}$ plotted for small roast and 3$\frac{2}{3}$ plotted for large roast; 1$\frac{1}{3}$ hours (The work may describe using the number line to find the difference, or could show the calculation 3$\frac{2}{3}$ − 2$\frac{1}{3}$ = 1$\frac{1}{3}$.)

Quiz 41: Solving Area Problems

1. D **2.** B **3.** $(6 \times 6) - (4 \times 2) = 28$; 28 square units **4.** 22 cm² **5.** 1st, 4th, 5th **6.** 3 inches; $2 \times 3 = 6$, $4 \times 3 = 12$, $6 \times 3 = 18$, $9 \times 3 = 27$ **7.** 32, 10, 8, 40; 1 by 640 meters, 2 by 320 meters, 4 by 160 meters, or 5 by 128 meters (The student may use equations like $128 \times 5 = 640$ or describe finding factor pairs of 640.) **8.** 5 by 9 rectangle, 45 cm²; 7 by 8 rectangle, 8 cm; 3 by 6 rectangle, 3 cm **9.** 8, 168 ($150 \div 21 = 7$ r 3, so needs 8 to have over 150 square feet. Total area $= 8 \times 21 = 168$.) **10.** 16 by 3, 12 by 4, and 8 by 6 rectangles drawn; length 16 in., width 3 in., area 48 in.²; length 12 in., width 4 in., area 48 in.²; length 8 in., width 6 in., area 48 in.²

Quiz 42: Solving Perimeter Problems

1. B **2.** C **3.** D **4.** 3rd, 5th **5.** 3 cm **6.** 64, 24, 16, 13, 134, 75, 12 **7.** grids have a 7 by 1 and a 5 by 3 rectangle; $2 \times (6 + 2) = 16$ or $6 + 6 + 2 + 2 = 16$; $2 \times (7 + 1) = 16$ or $7 + 7 + 1 + 1 = 16$; $2 \times (5 + 3) = 16$ or $5 + 5 + 3 + 3 = 16$ **8.** 74 meters (The work may show adding the missing dimensions to the diagram or may show the calculation $28 + 6 + 6 + 6 + 6 + 3 + 3 + 16 = 74$.) **9.** 6 rolls of ribbon, 20 inches of ribbon left over (Perimeter $= 20 + 20 + 45 + 45 = 130$ inches. She needs 6 rolls of ribbon for at least 130 inches. $6 \times 25 = 150$, $150 - 130 = 20$.) **10.** 8 by 1, 7 by 2, 6 by 3, and 5 by 4 rectangles drawn; 5 feet by 4 feet (The work may show using the diagram to compare areas, or may calculate the areas to compare them.)

Quiz 43: Displaying Measurement Data in Line Plots

1. D **2.** points plotted: 2 points for $1\frac{3}{4}$, 3 points for 2, 1 point for $2\frac{1}{4}$, 5 points for $2\frac{1}{2}$, 1 point for $2\frac{3}{4}$, 1 point for 3 **3.** points plotted: 2 points for $3\frac{1}{8}$, 1 point for $3\frac{1}{4}$, 2 points for $3\frac{3}{8}$, 2 points for $3\frac{1}{2}$, 1 point for $3\frac{5}{8}$, 2 points for $3\frac{3}{4}$ **4.** points plotted: 1 point for $1\frac{1}{2}$, 3 points for $1\frac{3}{4}$, 1 point for 2, 4 points for $2\frac{1}{4}$, 2 points for $2\frac{1}{2}$, 3 points for $2\frac{3}{4}$; 10 days; $2\frac{1}{4}$ inches **5.** scale from 4 to 5 in increments of $\frac{1}{8}$; points plotted: 2 points for 4, 2 points for $4\frac{1}{8}$, 4 points for $4\frac{1}{4}$, 1 point for $4\frac{3}{8}$, 1 point for $4\frac{1}{2}$, 3 points for $4\frac{5}{8}$, 4 points for $4\frac{3}{4}$, 2 points for $4\frac{7}{8}$, 1 point for 5

Quiz 44: Using Line Plots to Solve Problems

1. B **2.** $2\frac{1}{4}$ miles ($1\frac{3}{4} + 2\frac{1}{4} + 2\frac{3}{4} + 3 = 9\frac{3}{4}$, $12 - 9\frac{3}{4} = 2\frac{1}{4}$ or $12 - 1\frac{3}{4} - 2\frac{1}{4} - 2\frac{3}{4} - 3 = 2\frac{1}{4}$) **3.** point added for $11\frac{3}{4}$; $10\frac{1}{2} + 12\frac{3}{4} + 11\frac{3}{4} = 35$ **4.** $\frac{1}{10}$; $\frac{3}{10}$; $\frac{5}{10}$ or $\frac{1}{2}$ **5.** points plotted: 5 points for 2, 1 point for $2\frac{3}{4}$, 1 point for 3; $2\frac{3}{4}$ inches and 3 inches; The student should explain that it is possible, and tell how 7 days of $2\frac{1}{4}$ inches of rain would have a total of $15\frac{3}{4}$ inches. **6.** $\frac{6}{8}$ or $\frac{3}{4}$ ounces ($3\frac{7}{8} - 3\frac{1}{8} = \frac{6}{8} = \frac{3}{4}$); $\frac{3}{8}$ ounces ($3\frac{3}{4} - 3\frac{3}{8} = 3\frac{6}{8} - 3\frac{3}{8} = \frac{3}{8}$); any list of 3 of the measurements that have a sum of 10, such as $3\frac{1}{4}$, $3\frac{1}{4}$, and $3\frac{1}{2}$ or $3\frac{1}{8}$, $3\frac{3}{8}$, and $3\frac{1}{2}$

Quiz 45: Understanding Angles and Angle Measurement

1. A **2.** C **3.** D **4.** Greater than 180°; Less than 90°; Between 90° and 180°; Between 90° and 180°; Less than 90°; Greater than 180° **5.** 75° angle drawn; 110° angle drawn; 195° angle drawn; 230° angle drawn; 265° angle drawn; 325° angle drawn **6.** 94° (The student may explain that the two angles will add to 360°, or could use the equation 360 − 266 = 94.) **7.** 72° (The student may explain that the five equal angles will add to 360°, or could use the equation 360 ÷ 5 = 72.)

Quiz 46: Measuring Angles

1. 28°, 34°, 43°, 72°, 98°, 125°, 152°, 158° **2.** 90°, 55°, 35°; 90°, 60°, 30°; 90°, 38°, 52°; 90°, 42°, 48°; All the triangles have a 90° angle or a right angle. **3.** 103° and 77°; 76° and 104°; 119° and 59°; 60° and 120° **4.** hexagon labeled with the angles 111°, 127°, 139°, 105°, 142° and 96°

Note: angle measurements for Quiz 46 may vary by 1 or 2 degrees

Quiz 47: Sketching Angles

1. angles sketched with measures of 25°, 40°, 82°, 94°, 105°, 136°, 152°, 172° **2.** triangle sketched with angles of 90°, 20°, and 70° **3.** trapezoid sketched with two adjacent angles of 120° and two adjacent angles of 60° **4.** rhombus sketched with two opposite angles of 45° and two opposite angles of 135° **5.** pentagon sketched with 5 equal angles of 108° **6.** two angles sketched with measures between 145° and 150° **7.** 100° angle sketched

Quiz 48: Decomposing Angles

1. C **2.** B **3.** B **4.** 140°, 102°, 67°, 62° **5.** angle divided into two equal parts; 40°; 40° + 40° = 80° **6.** angle divided into four equal parts; 35°; 35° + 35° + 35° + 35° = 140° **7.** 180 − 35 − 80 = 65; 65° **8.** 40° (360 − 130 − 50 − 50 − 90 = 40)

Quiz 49: Solving Problems Involving Angles

1. B **2.** D **3.** A **4.** C **5.** 21° and 69°, 62° and 28°; any three angles with a sum of 90° (such as 21° and 25° and 44° or 44° and 37° and 9°); 143° and 37°; any three angles with a sum of 180° (such as 44° and 9° and 127° or 138° and 33° and 9°) **6.** straight angle divided into angles of 105°, 35°, and 40° **7.** 140° (360 − 87 − 53 − 80 = m or 87 + 53 + 80 + m = 360) **8.** triangle divided in two with a vertical line down the center; 90° and 72° and 18° **9.** 90° and 37° and 53° (first angle found as 180 − 143 = 37; right angle is 90°; final angle found as 180 − 37 − 90 = 53) **10.** c = 64°, d = 116° (c = 90 − 26 = 64; d = 180 − 64 = 116)

Quiz 50: Finding the Area of Complex Shapes

1. C **2.** B **3.** C **4.** $(1 \times 2) + (8 \times 5)$, $(3 \times 5) + (3 \times 7)$, $(2 \times 5) + (5 \times 3)$, $(3 \times 8) + (4 \times 3)$ **5.** 6 by 2 and 4 by 3 rectangle combined in any way, 5 by 2 and 3 by 3 rectangle combined in any way, 8 by 1 and 2 by 4 rectangle combined in any way **6.** 5 by 4 and 8 by 2 rectangle combined in any way; 36 square feet **7.** $111 (The student may find the area and cost for each rectangle and add them [$9 \times 3 = 27$, $27 \times 3 = 81$, $2 \times 5 = 10$, $10 \times 3 = 30$, $81 + 30 = 111$]. The student may find the combined area and then the cost [$(9 \times 3) + (5 \times 2) = 37$, $37 \times 3 = 111$]) **8.** 88 square meters (The student could use the equation $(10 \times 4) + (6 \times 8) = 88$, or could show finding the area of each rectangle separately and adding them.); 192 square meters (The student could use the equation $(20 \times 14) - 88 = 192$, or could show finding the total area and then subtracting the area of the pool.) **9.** 32 square feet (The student could use the equation $4 \times 8 = 32$, could count by 4s, or could give a written explanation.)

Quizzes 51 to 56: Geometry

Quiz 51: Identifying and Drawing Points, Lines, Line Segments, and Rays

1. D **2.** A **3.** 1st, 4th **4.** (left to right, top to bottom) endpoint, line segment, point, ray **5.** Rays and line segments both have an endpoint.; Rays have an endpoint on only one end, while line segments have endpoints on both ends. OR Rays continue in one direction without ending.; Rays have an endpoint, while lines do not. OR Rays continue in one direction, while lines continue in both directions. **6.** points C and D plotted, all points connected to form square ABCD with side lengths of 6 units **7.** Y and Z drawn 8 units apart and connected with a straight line segment; line segment; It has two endpoints, so is a line segment. **8.** line segment connecting A and B; line passing through B and C and continuing both up and down; ray with an endpoint at C continuing to the left; ray with an endpoint at A continuing down **9.** line has arrows at both ends; ray has endpoint at one end and arrow at the other; line segment has endpoints at both ends

Quiz 52: Identifying and Drawing Angles

1. D **2.** B **3.** 5 **4.** 1st, 3rd, 6th **5.** all angles less than 90° circled (2 each on first five shapes, 4 on last shape) **6.** any angle less than 90°, <; any angle between 90° and 180°, >, <; 90° angle, = **7.** any triangle with one obtuse angle; any triangle with three acute angles; any quadrilateral with two obtuse and two acute angles; trapezoid with two right, one acute, and one obtuse angle

Quiz 53: Identifying and Drawing Perpendicular and Parallel Lines

1. D **2.** A **3.** A **4.** line drawn crossing the first line at 90°; 90° **5.** line drawn crossing the first line, but not at 90°; Two acute angles and two obtuse angles are formed. **6.** triangle ABC divided with a vertical line; triangle XYZ divided with a horizontal line **7.** The student should explain that none of the lines are parallel because they are not always the same distance apart or because they will all meet or intersect at some point.; The student should explain that none of the lines are perpendicular because none intersect at a right angle. **8.** The student should explain that Pair 2 are not parallel because they will meet and intersect at some point. **9.** The student should identify that the rhombus and the square have perpendicular diagonals, and describe how the diagonals intersect at right angles. **10.** Q and T, R and S; Q and P, T and P

Quiz 54: Classifying Two-Dimensional Figures

1. B **2.** A **3.** C **4.** 4th, 6th **5.** square, rectangle, trapezoid, right triangle **6.** trapezoid, right triangle **7.** The student should identify that all the shapes in Group A have equal side lengths or equal angles, while the shapes in Group B have different side lengths or different angles. **8.** right triangle has 1st and 2nd ticked; rectangle has all ticked; trapezoid has 3rd ticked; square has all ticked **9.** D, F, H, I; D, F, H, I; A, C, D, E, F, H, J **10.** any rhombus, rhombus; any right triangle, right triangle **11.** any equilateral triangle drawn; The student should identify that the angles are equal. The student may explain the answer by measuring the angles and stating that they are all 60°, or by explaining that a triangle with 3 equal sides also has 3 equal angles.

Quiz 55: Understanding Symmetry

1. C **2.** A **3.** 1st, 2nd, 4th, 5th, 6th **4.** each diagram is completed with the mirror image of the shape across the line **5.** each diagram is completed with the mirror image of the shape across the line **6.** each diagram is completed with the mirror image of the shape across the lines **7.** The student should identify that the block pattern has symmetry. The student may identify the vertical or horizontal lines of symmetry, or may explain that one half is the mirror image of the other. **8.** A horizontal line should be drawn along the center of the shape; The student should explain that the two halves will fit exactly on each other or will have no overlap when folded.

Quiz 56: Identifying and Drawing Lines of Symmetry

1. D **2.** A **3.** C **4.** A **5.** 2 **6.** four lines of symmetry drawn (one vertical, one horizontal, and two diagonal) **7.** A, M, T, V, and Y have vertical lines of symmetry drawn; C, D, and E have horizontal lines of symmetry; X may have a vertical or a horizontal line of symmetry **8.** The student should identify that the octagon has the most lines of symmetry. The student may describe drawing the lines of symmetry on the shapes, or may identify that the pentagon has 5, the hexagon has 6, and the octagon has 8. **9.** The student should identify that Jade is not correct. The student may explain that the two parts are not mirror images or do not fit on each other with no overlap. **10.** parallelogram; 4; 2; 1 **11.** B; A; C and D; The student should explain that there is no way to fold the triangle with no overlap or that there is no way to draw a line where each side is a mirror image of the other.

Made in the USA
Columbia, SC
12 April 2022